THE KIDS' FAMILY TREE BOOK

Caroline Leavitt

Illustrated by Ian Phillips

Sterling Publishing Co., Inc.
New York

Special thanks are due to all those—family and friends—who provided information and gave permission for the use of many old and perhaps slightly more recent photographs in this book. Your help was invaluable.

Edited by Claire Bazinet
Design by Judy Morgan and Lucy Wilner

Library of Congress Cataloging-in-Publication Data Available

2 4 6 8 10 9 7 5 3 1
Published by Sterling Publishing Co., Inc.
387 Park Avenue South, New York, NY 10016
© 2005 by Caroline Leavitt
Distributed in Canada by Sterling Publishing
℅ Canadian Manda Group, 165 Dufferin Street
Toronto, Ontario, Canada M6K 3H6
Distributed in Great Britain and Europe by Chris Lloyd at Orca Book
Services, Stanley House, Fleets Lane, Poole BH15 3AJ, England
Distributed in Australia by Capricorn Link (Australia) Pty. Ltd.
P.O. Box 704, Windsor, NSW 2756, Australia

Sterling ISBN 1-4027-0942-0

For information about custom editions, special sales, premium and
corporate purchases, please contact Sterling Special Sales
Department at 800-805-5489 or specialsales@sterlingpub.com.

CONTENTS

FOREWORD

Do you have a family tree? No, don't look around for a big trunk topped with green leaves. That's not the kind of tree we're talking about. When you are born, you become a living and growing part of your own family tree. Your parents and brothers and sisters, and your aunts and uncles and other relatives, all play their parts in helping the branches of your family tree spread out and grow strong. Are you ready to put them in their honored places in your family tree? It's time to learn about and meet your ancestors. And it all begins with a word you may have heard: genealogy.

Chapter 1
GENEALOGY IS YOU!

WHAT MAKES YOU YOU?

Ever wonder how you became who you are?
Why you are tall or short? How your hair
got to be curly or straight? Your skin dark
or pale or olive?

How you got to be the way you are is
due, in large part, to your family genealogy.
Look at members of your family and you
might notice things you all share, beyond
the same last name and hometown. Your
father might be tall the way you are and
have the same springy dark hair. Your
mother's brown eyes might be the same
chocolate shade as yours. If you have
siblings, maybe your brother has your same
strong nose, or your sister shares your
lopsided smile. If you are one of identical twins, it's like looking in a mirror!

It's not only "looks" that families share. Talents, such as a beautiful singing voice
or being able to draw wonderful pictures, can also run in families. So can medical
problems, such as being colorblind or sneezing around cats or dogs or at certain
times of the year. You might also be much different in some ways from your parents
and your siblings. Maybe you are short while they are all tall or you enjoy telling
long involved stories, but your dad can't even tell a joke!

And then there's what you're like on the inside. Where do you get your personality? Do you like to sit quietly in a chair and read, lost for hours the way your mother does? Do you love the beach the way your cousins do? Or yearn to be a doctor like your dad? Are you more like your aunt than your mother? How so? Who shares what? Are there more people in your family who like to paint than who like to write? Who has the good sense of humor? Who is quick to anger? Do you have a temper, too? Has someone asked, "Who do you take after?" It's really a good question. Do you know the answer?

Knowing about your family can help you to learn a whole lot more about yourself. Knowing about your ancestors' place in their world can help you to understand your place in yours.

IT'S NOT ALL MOM AND DAD

How you got to be you doesn't stop with just your immediate family. Maybe no one in your family now may be tall like you, but maybe your great-uncle was six feet tall. And his father before him might have been six feet five! Of course, if you are adopted, you may not look anything like the family you know and love. You may have your birth mother's flaming red hair or your birth father's love of math.

Your family genes stretch far back, further than anybody remembers. Think about it. Your mother had a mother, and her mother had a mother, and her mother had a mother, and her mother, too. Going back several generations, your great-grandfather's great-grandfather might have been a shoemaker in England. Your great-grandmother's

Could this baby on her grandfather's knee be your great grandmother? ▼

It's always good to gather four generations together for a photo.

6

great-grandmother might have been making lasagna (a noodle and sauce dish) in Italy or borscht (a tasty beet soup) in Russia. All these people could be a part of your family tree! And it's exciting to discover how these blood relations were like you, and how they were different.

THE GENES IN YOUR JEANS

The important part of the word genealogy, which means the study of family history, is gene. Genes are the materials in every cell of your body that give instructions to your body for creating the one and only special you. No one is exactly like you (only identical twins are the same). Genes are carried on tiny structures called chromosomes. Every cell in your body has 46 chromosomes that come in pairs of 23 each. Inside the chromosomes is your DNA (short for a word that's a real mouthful: deoxyribonucleic acid), and this DNA is what gives your body the messages to create you.

You received your chromosomes—and your genes—from your parents: some from your father and some from your mother. Before you were born, they blended together and created a blueprint for the person you would be. So, your parents got their genes from their parents (your mother from her mother and father, and your father from his mother and father). And those people, your grandparents, got their genes from your great-grandparents. I'm sure you can guess now where your great-grandparents got their genes. And aren't you getting excited about finally finding out just who all those people were and what they were like?

Genes dictate lots of things. Think of your extended family—your uncles, aunts, and grandparents. If they share the same big ears or deep voice, you can credit it to genes. But remember, not everyone will have the same family look, because your uncle may be part of your family "by marriage" not by blood, because he married your mother's sister. His genes come from a totally different family.

WHY STUDY GENEALOGY?

Study genealogy and you will probably find yourself traveling to other times and other lands. You might discover that an ancestor on your father's side was a famous admiral. Maybe someone on your mother's side was a photographer who traveled all over the world! Discovering the occupations and abilities about your ancestors can open up whole new worlds for you. The more you know about your family and your past, the more you might discover about yourself. If a great-aunt was an important political speaker, maybe the power to lead is in your blood, too, and you can achieve much more than you ever thought you could! If a great-great-grandfather was a celebrated opera singer, maybe you should reconsider your shyness about joining the school chorus or try *a capella* singing!

Genealogy can help you discover your family's place in the world. And yours.

Chapter 2
GETTING STARTED

YOUR FAMILY HISTORY

Did you ever hear someone say, "I know you like a book?" Well, imagine that your family history is a book. It's the story of how you got where you are, filled with photographs and stories of long-ago family members growing up, and maps of where they lived. It begins way back when, with your great-great-great-grandmother, and continues all the way down to you! Having a family scrapbook is a great way to know and understand your family. And knowing your family history is to really know yourself.

Your family history scrapbook will come, in time. For now, keep an eye out for a big scrapbook to buy, or put it on your gift "wish list." You'll want to set aside a page (or two or three) for each family member, starting with the oldest, say, your great-great-grandfather, and moving down to the youngest, which might be you. To fill up this "family story" book, you'll need to collect information on each person, including photographs and special keepsakes, which you can later paste into your family scrapbook. Imagine! Under a picture of your grandmother, for example, you might have information on when and where she was born, what school she went to, who she married, her likes and dislikes, and her famous apple pie recipe. Try to include other family "treasures," too, things that will remind you of her, such as a copy of her favorite joke, a report card, or a square cut from a dress she had when she was your age. All of these things, pasted into your scrapbook, will some day create a wonderful memory book to keep and display!

But before you can work on putting together your family scrapbook, you have to start gathering information—and have a place to put it!

Starting off right

To start your genealogy research, you will need a few supplies right away:

- some small notebooks—you should carry one with you at all times to make notes whenever you run across some great information.
- sharpened pencils—be sure to keep a couple handy. Shorter stubs are less likely to break.
- a loose-leaf binder and paper—you need a place to collect and keep all the information you turn up. When you get information on someone, put his or her name at the top of a page. Write the information on the page, and keep the page in the binder. Each time you get new information, add it to the right person's page. Soon this loose-leaf binder will be your best friend: a genealogy workbook that will help you keep track of your family tree.

THOSE FAMILY PHOTOS

Once you show an interest in genealogy, you can be sure that someone is going to drag out an old dusty album of photographs. Actually, putting names and then facts and stories to the faces you see there is a good part of the fun. Soon, you'll feel you really know them: the girl on the old merry-go-round, the serious young man in the sailor hat, the father proudly showing off the family car (with running boards). Then there are those baby pictures, confirmation or bar mitzvah photos, and school and graduation pictures, too. You're sure to find yourself in there somewhere. The pictures in the album may not mean much to you now, but they will.

The important thing, right at the start, is to take good care of any photographs you want to look at or borrow to copy for your genealogy projects. Try not to touch the picture part itself, only the edges. Depending on the age and kind of paper the pictures are printed on, even oil from your fingers could damage them. Most of the older photographs that you will find in family albums will be the only copy anyone has. If they are damaged or lost, they can't be replaced, so you'll need to make copies if you want to cut, pin up, or glue any pictures. And if you borrow any, be sure to return them in the same condition. You don't want to have a family feud on your hands!

Fun facts

- Tintypes, the first "instant" photographs, were inexpensive and unbreakable. They were made out of metal!
- Stereoscopic pictures were two photos of the same thing placed side by side. With a stereoscopic viewer, you saw the picture in 3-D!

*A tintype ▲
from the 1890's.*

◄ *A common
stereoscope.*

Chapter 3

YOUR FAMILY TREE

A family tree, as we said, isn't a tree but a kind of map. Instead of showing miles, a family tree shows how family members are related to one another. It can go back over many years; from you to your great-grandparents and beyond. The family tree form is called that because of the way it shows family members "branching out" from one another, like tree branches are connected to each other and to the trunk of the tree.

MAPPING YOUR FAMILY

Are you ready to begin drawing your family tree? Do you have enough information to begin? Yes, at least to start. You know who you are, and how you are related to your mother and your father (you are their child). And you know how you are related to your grandparents, your mother and father's parents. So, let's start you off with a really simple family tree.

1. Find a large piece of paper, make a circle near the bottom and inside write your full name (first, middle, and last). Under your name, put your birth date (month, day, and year).

2. Make two lines going upward and draw two more circles at the top, like balloons. In one, write in your mother's full name and her birth date. Write your father's full name in the other. Put in his birth date, too. (Ask for the correct spelling and birth dates.)

3. Make more lines going upward (more balloons): two from your mother's circle and two from your father's circle. Top each of them with two more circles. In these circles, write in your grandparents' full names—your mother's mother and father above her circle and your father's mother and father above his circle. Put in their birth dates.

That's a good start. Next, if you have brothers and sisters, and aunts and uncles, and cousins, you'll want to add them to your family tree, too. Your brothers and sisters are your siblings, which means that they are your parents' children, too. And your cousins are the children of your aunts and uncles. So they'll be listed on the family tree under their parents. This means you'll need a much bigger piece of paper, or some type of pedigree or genealogy form, to keep track of everybody!

Family tree tips

List each person in your family tree, then try to find out:
- when the person was born. Where.
- what schools the person went to. Years graduated.
- where the person lived.
- what jobs the person held.
- if a person was in the military. What service, where and when.
- if a person emigrated. From where and when.
- if the person is dead. When. Where. How. Where buried.

How much of this or other information you will want to put into your family tree diagram is up to you. But don't miss out on gathering the information while you can, so you can record it in your loose-leaf binder and later in your family scrapbook.

GROWING YOUR FAMILY TREE

Even if you start small, remember that big family trees grow from tiny roots. Here is a part of a family tree form. At the top would be the oldest relatives that you know, probably your grandparents. Vertical and horizontal lines map out your parents and their siblings, and you and your siblings, if you have them. Remember, you have two sets of grandparents—your mother's parents and your father's parents. That means you'll have eight great-grandparents. Your family tree will grow quickly once you start, so every time you learn about a relative, add his or her name to your family tree form, along with important vital statistics such as birth, marriage and death dates. When you hear or find new stories about a relative, write them all down in your loose-leaf notebook. By the time you're finished, you should have a huge family tree that you can frame and hang in your room and a notebook filled with lots of family facts.

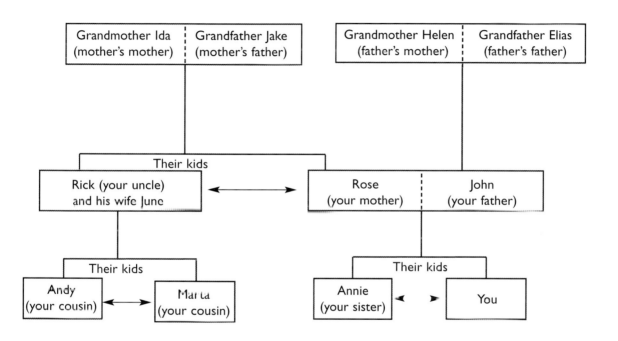

From this diagram it's easy to see how people in your family are related. Horizontal boxes side by side mean the people are siblings (brothers and sisters). Vertical lines tell us descent (who is the parent and who is the child). You can also see that your maternal grandmother and grandfather were married and had two kids.

With this kind of system, you can easily add more information. For example: Next to or beneath each name, you might write B (for birth) and D (for death) and put in the dates—at least the year, although the place is important, too. If the person is still living (such as you are, of course) put a small dash after the birth date. For example, if your birth year is 1995, you would write B1995–. Later on, after you've done some detective work, you'll have a lot more information to add.

If you want more information, write in M (for married) and the date. How would you show if someone was divorced? Since "D" stands for death, you can put a slash through the M and add the divorce date for M̸ 1982–1991.

BRINGING YOUR FAMILY TO LIFE

As you learn more about your family, you'll find yourself really getting to know them. You'll want to write down where family members were born, and when and where they got married (if they did). You will definitely want to add when, where, and how the person died (if they are no longer living), and where they are buried. People often make visits to the graves of family members on the departed relative's birthday or on the anniversary of their death. This is a good time for you to go, too. The person's full name and birth and death dates are etched on the cemetery gravestones. Be sure to bring one of your small notebooks and a pencil or two and take down the information. You may need it to order a death certificate or find an obituary.

Death certificates are official papers issued at the time of death. If your family doesn't have a death certificate for a deceased grandparent, you should be able to order a copy for a fee from the local courthouse where the person lived, or from the Office or Bureau of Vital Statistics. You'll need the full name and year and place of death, and a reason for requesting the certificate. Obituaries are much easier to find and often provide much more information.

An obituary is a short biography about the person who has died. Local newspapers print obituaries to tell their readers (often friends and neighbors of the deceased) that the person has passed away. Newspapers keep archives of everything they print. If you know the date a person died, you can search the archives of the local newspaper for that person's obituary. It is usually printed in an issue a day or two later. Libraries sometimes keep microfilm archives of old issues of local papers. An obituary can provide a lot of helpful information when you are researching your family tree.

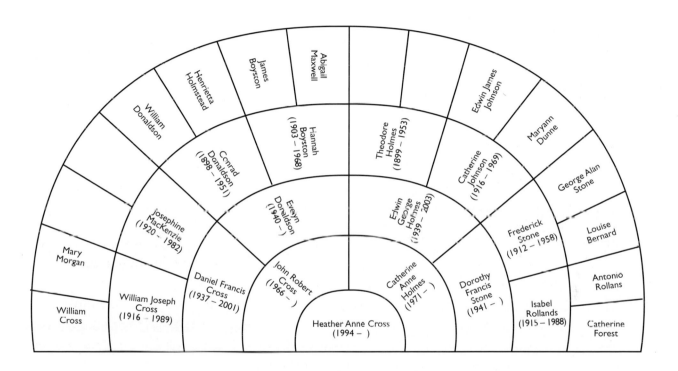

A fan-shaped pedigree chart such as this one is a good way to keep track of, and display, just your direct-line ancestors, rather than all family members. It is easy to see how several generations all come down to you.

PEDIGREE CHART

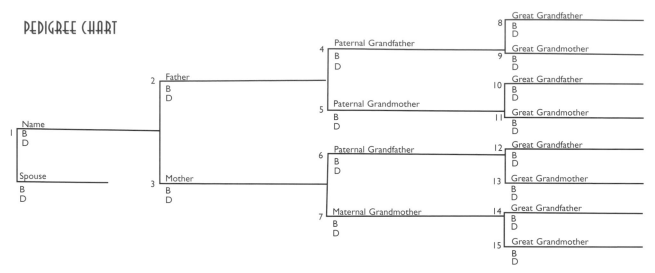

Key

Born
Married
Died
Cemetery/**C**hildren

This type of pedigree form gives you room under the name line for important family details: date and place of birth, death, marriage; where buried, children's names, etc.

It can be extended as far back in time as you have room on the paper. If each ancestor on the chart is numbered, it is easy to key file folders to the chart, then arrange the folders accordingly.

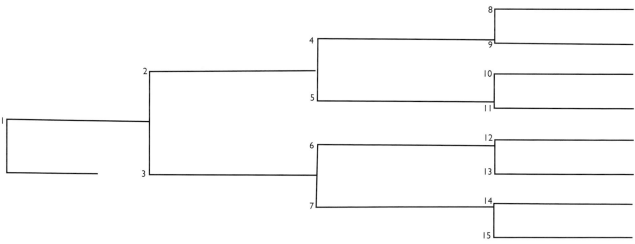

Chapter 4

DIGGING FOR YOUR ROOTS

$\mathcal{B}$efore you get to know your ancestors, let's start with the person and the people you know best—you and your immediate family! The answers you find here will start you on your genealogical trail.

HOW TO DO RESEARCH

Finding out facts about your family involves research. The first and easiest way to get some answers is simply by asking yourself some questions, or by interviewing your parents. This is called using primary sources, primary meaning "first." These are the people in your immediate family: your father and mother, yourself and your older siblings. Start by finding out the basic facts—names, dates, places. Later on, when you've figured out who everybody is, you can go back to people and collect family stories, called recording "oral history." In the meantime, if you do need to get some quieter relatives talking, asking a few of the questions on page 69 (taking oral histories) might help to draw them out.

START WITH WHAT YOU KNOW

You may be surprised to discover just how much important information about yourself you already know, and how much you need to find out. You probably know what your name is and where you were born. But maybe you don't know your middle name (or names) or the exact time of your birth—a fun thing to know. So ask your parents to see and help you make a copy of your birth certificate. Certificates are official records used in keeping track of what happens in people's lives. There are certificates for birth, baptism, marriage, and death. Each of these certificates can offer a wealth of information about you, and about the people in your family tree.

Watch for treasure

As you research and do your interviews, keep an eye and ear out for these great sources of information:

1. Marriage license—where and when a family member was married.

2. Diploma—where and when someone earned a degree.

3. Death certificate or newspaper obituary notice—where and when someone died (sometimes how or why they died). Also, where they are buried, and what family members survived him or her.

4. Family Bible—births, marriages and deaths may be recorded and the Bible handed down from generation to generation. A wonderful family heirloom.

5. Personal diaries and letters—names of family and friends (who could have important information), places the family might have lived (look at return address), important details of daily lives and wonderful stories of the times in which the people lived.

6. Internet—all manner of information: more is being added and made available daily.

BEGIN AT THE BEGINNING

Birth records generally include the name of the child and the parents, and the exact date and even time of birth. The name of the hospital is there, too, and the signature of the doctor in charge. You might find some funny things, too, such as a footprint taken right after the baby was born, or a few strands of hair stuck to it.

Look at your birth certificate and you may notice that the name you've always used isn't exactly the one you were given at birth. If people call you Harry, your birth name may actually be Henry or Harold. Peggy is a common nickname for Margaret, but Peggy could actually be the name given on the birth certificate, not Margaret. Someone called Max might have been named Maximilian, after a long-ago Roman emperor, or Maxine!

As you search out old birth certificates, you might be surprised to find a person's last name isn't the same as on their birth certificate. It could be a simple spelling mistake, or that the person disliked the name so changed it. Sometimes, a name was simplified or changed when an immigrant moved to a new country with a different language and culture (Sandlovitz might have been shortened to Sands, while Roi (in French) was translated to King in English).

Time out for a holiday photo with visiting cousins.

LET'S TALK

Now that you've found out some basic family facts, you're ready to learn about interviewing. But asking questions, even of people you know well, isn't always easy. You'll need to know what questions to ask and how to ask them to get the answers you want. Where do you start?

Think. Now that you have some information on family members, who do you think might be the most helpful? How about some of the oldest? Do you have several relatives who are about the same age, in their 60s or 70s, or maybe older?

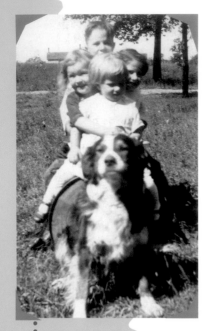

Lucky you! These are the family members you want to talk to and interview as quickly as you can. They could be a great help to you in your genealogy search. Their stories of who their parents and grandparents were, where they came from, and how things were when they were kids are there waiting to be told.

But people are different. Some are willing to talk about just anything for hours, while others need to be put at ease before they will open up to you. During an interview, one person will answer questions with only a word or two, so you'll need to ask follow-up questions to get the information you're looking for. Another person will ramble on with a long involved story instead of telling you what you want to know. You need to take control the interview and bring the talkative ones back on track.

It's nice ▲
to have the
family dog in
the picture.

SETTING UP AN INTERVIEW

To get ready to interview, before you sit down to questions, you'll need some way to catch and keep their responses, and whatever else they may say. A good way is to use a tape recorder (remember to use fresh batteries). That way, you'll have a record of any valuable information, and be able to listen to it again and again to refresh your memory. After the interview, you'll want to "transcribe" or copy the words onto paper to have easy access to it. If someone objects or is clearly uncomfortable being tape recorded, go back to that old standby of information gathering—a notebook and a few pencils or pens.

ASKING QUESTIONS!

To make your researches easier and later organize the information in your workbook, it helps to have a form that can be filled out. Then you can be sure to ask the same questions of everyone you interview. For relatives who don't live nearby, the form can be sent in the mail (or by e-mail) with a note attached. Explain what you are doing and that you'd like each family member to fill out the form for you. Ask if they would "please" send back the filled-out form by a certain date (allowing two weeks or so is about right). That way the form is less likely to be set aside and forgotten, or mislaid. Copy this form, or make up one of your own:

1. **Full name** (first, middle, last)

2. **Date and place of birth**

3. **Father's name**

4. **Mother's maiden name**

5. **Current address**

6. **Past addresses** (when moved)

7. **Education** (when, where)

8. **Health problems**

9. **Employment**

10. **Married** (name, date, place)

11. **Children** (name, date, place born)

12. **Divorced** (name, date, place)

13. **Military service** (when, branch of service)

14. **Awards and honors received**

15. **Memberships** (club, church, organization)

16. **Pets**

17. **Special talents**

Is there anything else about yourself that you would like me to know?

Who else should receive a copy of this form (name, relationship, address)?

Asking the final questions above might get you some information you wouldn't have thought to ask about and leads to family members you don't know well. Add new names to your list of relatives to be interviewed or sent a copy of the form. It's a good idea, too, to leave space at the bottom of your form for any "Comments" or "Stories." If room is tight on the form, suggest that additional information be written on the back of the form or on a separate sheet. Note: Remember to ask each relative for a nice close-up photo (a head shot) that you can keep.

HOW FAR BACK CAN YOU GO?

It's thrilling to have all that information coming in! As the forms are filled out or returned, use a three-hole punch along the left side and put the pages into your loose-leaf binder. Add only basic facts (such as birth date) to your working family tree. Later, you'll use a lot more of this helpful and interesting information in making up your family history scrapbook. For now, keep the forms all neat and safe in one handy place, your loose-leaf genealogy workbook.

BE PREPARED!

Even when you are not planning to interview someone, keep a small notebook and a couple of sharp pencils or pens with you at all times. You never know when you might need it! At a family dinner, your father might start talking about the time his uncle won first prize in a yodeling contest. Or, you could be driving home with your mother when she starts telling you about how her grandfather won a lot of money in a lottery. Remember, when you record the information, write down who told you about it, and where and when you got the information (carry a small calendar so you can look up the date). Later, if you need to, you can go back to that person ("primary source") and ask for more information about a particular ancestor. Like the detectives on TV cop shows, whip out your notebook and jot things down. You can refer to them later, to jog your memory and your source's memory.

Genealogy work has its own language. Here is a list of vocabulary words that should help you in researching your family tree:

Ancestor—someone you are descended from—your parents' parents, their parents, and so on.

Archives—a collection of historical records and items: birth and death records, land deeds; back issues of old newspapers.

Autobiography—a life story, told by that person.

Biography—the life story of someone, told by someone else.

Census—an official count of residents (who they are, where they live) taken at certain times, such as every 10 years.

Descendant—someone who comes from you—your children, and their children.

Emigrate—to move from a country or a place to start a new life in a new country or place.

Fraternal—brothers born at same time (twins), but not from same egg (identical).

Genealogy—a "mapping" of family members, from the farthest back ancestor to the living members of the family.

Generation—family members on the same "step" of family history (great-grandparents, grandparents, parents).

Genes—biologically, what makes you who you are (DNA code).

Head of Household—the adult responsible for a family group.

Immigrant—a person who enters a country to stay and live permanently.

Maiden name—Surname of an unmarried woman, which may change at marriage.

Maternal—"from the mother." Relatives on your maternal side are directly related to your mother.

Paternal—"from the father." Relatives on your paternal side are directly related to your father.

Pedigree—a person's record, in chart form, of parental and ancestral information (Similar in meaning to genealogy).

Relatives—people who are directly related to you.

Sibling—a person's brother or sister.

Spouse—a person's husband or wife.

Surname—a person's last or "family" name.

Loving hugs unite the generations everywhere in the world.

Chapter 5
GETTING ORGANIZED

*R*emember that loose-leaf binder we suggested you get? You'll definitely want to have one specific place to keep it and all that family information you've been gathering. A big binder that you keep at home (you won't want to be carrying it around with you) is something you'll always be able to find. It will be your genealogical workbook, and hold tons of detailed information. Your family tree diagram just maps out your family relationships, but the information stored in your loose-leaf binder can be used to put together a family scrapbook: along with pictures, quotations from letters, and other interesting things you've discovered about family members.

YOUR GENEALOGICAL WORKBOOK

You can organize your loose-leaf genealogical workbook in different ways. The easiest way is to give family members their own page. Put the name of each family member at the top of a separate page. Right now, you probably know more about yourself than about any of your family members. So, start with your name, and set up the page in the binder so that when you open it, your page is on top. Next, put in a page for each of your siblings (sisters and brothers) if any, then your parents and their siblings (your aunts and uncles). (You will probably need to interview each of them to get information to fill in the pages.) After the pages for your aunts and uncles will come your grandparents' pages with their names at the top, and so on. This way, you can go back in time, from generation to generation, as far as your genealogical research takes you.

You will soon see, as you gather information and talk to and find out more about your relatives, that the information in your binder will grow and grow.

MORE ORGANIZATION TIPS

Your loose-leaf binder is your best friend. It's here where you'll rewrite neatly your scribbled interview notes or copy down your taped interviews. Be sure to write down the date of the interview, and the name of the person interviewed. You may have more questions to ask, or need to update your notes.

A blackboard with chalk, white board with erasable marker or, better yet, a cork bulletin board with index cards and pushpins comes in handy, too. You can post "things to be done"—such as family members to follow up on, as you do your research.

Pick up a set of brightly colored pens to color code your notes, using red for your mother's side of the family and blue for your father's side, for example.

Use stick-on notes to draw your attention and remind yourself of something you need to do more work on. Different color note sheets can help here, too.

A number of folders with a cardboard box to hold them makes a handy filing system. You can use different color folders (or markings or labels) for each side of your family, or for different generations, or you can invent a system that works for you.

Special occasion photos, like ▲ 50th wedding anniversaries, can help to fix the date of the picture.

GOOD WAYS TO KEEP "KEEPSAKES"

As you "grow" your family tree, you're going to run across items you'll want to keep. They won't fit in your binder and may even be too bulky for your scrapbook. Photo boxes, or plain old shoeboxes, make great catch-alls. They are perfect for envelopes of photos (remember to identify who's in the pictures), folded or rolled copies of birth and other certificates, expired passports and drivers' licenses. Letters from a homesick soldier, a child away at camp for the first time, or a stack of old love letters are wonderful family keepsakes. You'll want to hold onto military awards and medals, of course, but old school report cards are also fun to have. Note: If you need two or more boxes to hold everything, separate the contents and label or code the containers to make finding things easier.

KEEP THINGS TOGETHER

If paperwork and other keepsakes are piling up, designate a section of your room as your Genealogical Research Center. You might even want to put up a sign that says so. Keep any audio or video tapes you've made here, along with your filled notebooks (keep your current one with you at all times). Store your oversized or treasured photographs in sturdy flat boxes that will keep them safe, and odd-sized items neatly in photo or shoe boxes. Your looseleaf binder, or binders if you are using more than one, should be where they are easy to reach and work with. And don't forget—every time you gather a new piece of information, be sure to bring it right to this special area. A bulletin board is a good idea, so that small scribbled notes can be posted and won't become lost. It's a reminder, too, to follow-up or transfer the information later into your binder. Don't put it off too long, because that's how valuable information can get lost—and how a neat and tidy area can quickly morph into a messy one.

"My Family" Box

Why not consider a file-sized box, with separators and manila folders, to keep things in place? (You'll want to decorate it appropriately, of course.)

What You Need:
- box about 12" by 12" by 9" deep
- cardboard separators
- stick-on labels
- manila folders (with tabs)
- copies of photos, clippings, to decorate box
- glue
- scissors
- markers
- shellac
- small brush

What To Do:
1. Cut cardboard to fit box (12" by 9½"), for use as separators.
2. Use markers to print labels: Maternal Side, Paternal Side, Maternal Grandparents, Paternal Grandparents, etc.
3. Dot glue the tabs and attach them to the sides of the separators. Change the positions of each label so each heading will be visible!
4. Cut around the copies of family photos. Be sure to include ones from both your maternal (mother) and paternal (father) side of the family. Dot glue on the back of the photographs and paste them all over your box.
5. Dip your brush into the shellac and carefully paint over your photos and your box. This will give it a protective covering and a nice shine.

On manila folders, use a marker that makes the words really stand out. Write the person's name, and put papers relating to that person in the folder. If there is too much, put the person's name on the folder, and then add "birth certificate," "diary pages," or "army records." Whatever the document, there's always a chance it could get misfiled. But if the folder is clearly and neatly labeled, it's a snap to know, when you come across it, where it should go, and re-file it.

LABEL, LABEL, LABEL

You might want to invest in some labels to stick on the backs of photographs. Regular labels are made to stay on, and that is fine if the photographs are your own. If photographs are borrowed, use removeable labels to identify them, so you can return them in the same condition you received them. On the label, clearly identify the date, place, and person or persons in the photo (reading from left to right). Tip: Do this while you are looking at the photograph, and place the label on the photo after you write it all out. You are less likely to make a mistake in writing down the information, and there is less danger of damaging the photo from pressing too hard or having the ink bleed through to the photograph. Be sure ink is dry before "stacking" photos.

While we are talking about labels, don't forget to pick up some that will fit on whatever size audio tape cassettes you are using to do your interviewing. Once you have more than one or two cassettes, it will become increasingly hard to locate specific interviews when you want to find them.

CARING FOR PHOTOGRAPHS

There are photographs and there are photographs. If you've just handed out a dozen copies of your latest class picture to relatives, it's no big deal if one or more become misplaced or lost, or are accidentally torn or damaged. But if your grandaunt lets you borrow her only picture of her mother,

▲ *Turning sixteen has always been a reason to have a portrait taken.*

your great-grandmother, taken when she was a schoolgirl, so that you can make a copy, it's a different story. Lose it, and it's gone! Sticky fingerprints, ink from markers, spills, or creases from not handling it carefully can also destroy a cherished keepsake photo.

Photo handling tips

- Hold all photos by the edges. Try not to touch the picture itself.
- Put photographs in clean envelopes or inside a folded sheet of paper to protect them.
- When mailing or carrying photographs, add a stiff piece of cardboard backing to keep the photograph flat (older photographs can be especially fragile and easily creased).
- Be careful writing on the backs of photographs. Marker ink can soak into older paper, and writing with pen or pencil can make impressions that show through on the picture side (write on regular or removeable labels and attach them instead).
- Don't use tape on the front (picture side) of photographs (if necessary, for example to stop a tear from causing more damage, attach tape to the back).
- Definitely, don't cut up any one-of-a-kind photos or use them in any projects. Make copies!

FINDING YOUR PLACE

Papers and notepads and books-oh, my! At some point a bookmark—or several—might come in handy. Of course, you can use just about anything for a bookmark, but why not make special bookmarks, starring family members, for a cool way to mark your place in your genealogy research.

Where should you start? How about with you? Are you the baby of the family? The big sister? The pesky little brother? We all have roles to play, based on birth order and our position in the family (and many of us play those roles to the hilt). Show your place in the family. Search out a good photo of yourself and clip out of magazines some small pictures that say, "This is me!" If you're nuts about sports, decorate your bookmark with pictures of balls (soccer, baseball, football, tennis) or players in action. You're the "princess" of the family? Cut out a crown, or draw one, for your head. Some pasted-on "jewels" will also show your regal side. Small squares cut from blue jeans (if you're the rough-and-tumble sort) or bits of lace (for the more ladylike)—it's up to you.

Birthdays are happy occasions for keepsake photos.

A tintype photo keeps family very near throughout the years.

Family Bookmarks

This easy, creative activity is designed to help you get to know your family members better, and keep you organized too. And, of course, they would make great "thank you" gifts to send to those special people in your family who helped with your research.

What You Need:
- poster board
- scissors
- markers
- picture
- clippings, scraps, or small mementos
- glue

What To Do:

1. Cut the poster board to a good bookmark size, say 3" wide by 8" long.
2. Arrange the photo (or photos) with whatever else you choose. Adjust their positions until you are happy with how it looks.
3. Glue each piece to the bookmark. Once the front side is dry, you can decorate the back if you wish—or glue or tape a long piece of colorful ribbon or yarn to it. Now make some bookmarks showing other family members. The more the merrier!

Chapter 6
SEARCHING ONLINE

Suppose you've gathered information on your immediate family by asking your parents questions about yourself and your family. You've started a family tree and filled out some forms. Interview tapes have been labeled and written out for your binder. You and your parents have searched through family papers and records. Now you need to dig deeper and farther back in time. A lot of the information you are looking for won't be first hand from your own knowledge, or even information your parents know. Where do you go from here? The answer could be as near as your home computer or as far as your local library.

Just as your parents and relatives are your primary sources of genealogy information, searching records are your secondary sources. They will help you dig deeper, and go farther and farther back into time.

When it comes to those secondary sources for researching your family tree, your computer is a great help. On-line, you can find information, listings, even copies of documents, but you have to know how to search, what to look for, and where to look.

If you go on the Internet often, you probably have a favorite search engine. Search engines are special Internet programs that search for key words. It brings up any document on the World Wide Web (the "www" in Internet addresses) in which that key word appears. Depending on what you enter and search for, you might get no "hits" at all, or maybe there will be ten, or even two hundred sites where that word or phrase appears. Google.com and yahoo.com, are two of the popular search engines on the Internet.

STARTING THE "SEARCH"

Here is an example: Let's say your grandfather told you that his grandfather came to America in the early 1900s. You don't know the year, and you don't know how. First, you would go to your favorite search engine and type in his name. Put quotation marks around the name so the search engine will search for the first and last names together. Did you get any hits? Maybe not, or maybe you are surprised to see a list of several people with that name. Can you narrow the search? Check the details given: the year, the age of the person, where he came from or lived. If the names listed are clearly not your grandfather's grandfather, don't give up. Other search engines could have access to different information, and there are other places to search.

FINDING VITAL RECORDS

Where did he live and work, and when and where did he die? Your next stop is to search websites that provide free Vital Records information (many websites charge a fee for use, but allow you to "try it out" first). Vital Records are official records of birth, death, marriage, and divorce organized by state or county in the United States. Some of this information is also picked up by genealogical sites, such as familysearch.com, or ancestry.com. There you type in your relative's name and any other details that might be helpful in the search. But have patience. Searches can take some time, especially if you have to check different states or locate appropriate websites in different countries.

As you do your searches, you may come up with many bits of information about your relative. You may find his Social Security Number (available on the Internet after a person has passed away), his wife's name, where they were married, where they lived, and even his occupation—all terrific helps. If you can, print off the information for your binder. If not, write the results of your searches onto that relative's loose-leaf page, date it, and copy down the full website address at the top. (The website address is the long string of letters, periods, and slashes showing in the address window when the site is open on screen.)

CHECKING CENSUS RECORDS

Another "must" search for information on ancestors going back at least 70 years are census records. A census is a count of people who live in an area. These records are taken at certain times, generally every ten years, in countries around the world. Census takers go from door to door and fill in forms on every person living at that address. Sometimes, people are asked to fill out and send back census forms that they receive in the mail. So, if you search for and find a great-grandfather's name in the census records, you'll learn a lot of things about him, and about other family members living there at that time. Go to earlier and later census records, and you will be able to track changes in the family from census to census, such as new births (age 7 in 1830), and likely deaths (was 82 in 1830; in 1840 no longer living at that address), job changes, and much more.

In the United States, census records are available for every decade, or ten years, from 1790 to 1930. Information from some old census records may be found online. To actually see and examine a particular filled-out census form, you may need to go to a federal archive facility.

Offices in various parts of the country make these records available for genealogy research and other purposes.

Information available on census form:

- Road, street, number or name of house
- Name and surname of each person
- Relation to head of family
- Married, single, widowed
- Age last birthday
- Profession or occupation
- Employed, neither
- Where born

LINKING UP

As you do your research on the computer, you'll often find phrases or words high-lighted in another color or underlined. These are called "links." Click on these links and they will take you to other websites where you might find more information to speed you along in your search. If you are lucky enough to find yourself at a website with a whole lot of information on your family, don't lose it! Enter it as a "favorite" so the computer will make it available to you whenever you want to go back to it. It might be a good idea, too, to make a written note of it, just in case. Adding the website address to a loose-leaf or notebook page, or to a form that you have made up to organize your records, will keep it handy—in case you need to look up the site again, even if you are on a different computer.

PAY-FOR-INFORMATION SITES

In doing only a few searches, you will notice that some genealogical sites ask you to "sign in" and some have fees for using the site. Should you pay for access to infor-mation? That depends on how far you have gotten with your searches, and how important it is for you to have access to information that you can't seem to find elsewhere. Check with your parents. They might have other leads to finding what you are looking for.

If you are just starting out, it is much more fun to see just how far you can get on your own. Later, if and when you've hit a dead end, or there are "holes" in your research that you're dying to fill, your parents may feel that paying a small fee would be worth it. If so, test out a likely website if you can before signing up for the service. Some sites will let you do a few searches to give you an idea of what kind of information and how much, is available. Maybe a few minutes work will fill that "hole" in your research, without you having to plunk down a good part of your allowance or hard-earned cash.

THE BASICS OF SEARCHING

In case doing searches online is new to you, here are a few tips about how to go about it:

1. Connect search words in quotes; for example, "Clutters Boston" for a Clutter family who lived in Boston. The search engine will look for both "Clutters" and "Boston" together. That way you will avoid getting Closet "Clutters" or "Boston" Red Sox.

2. Don't bother with little words. Small, connecting words such as "the," "and," "or," are a waste of time. The search engine ignores them.

3. Be specific if you know details: your great-uncle was a member of "Knights of Columbus Baltimore 1900s." If you're not sure, search instead for "Men's Organizations Maryland 1900s" and check out the hits that come up.

Some Internet files can be very long, and would waste a lot of paper and printing ink if you printed them out. If you can, it's best to "copy" the information you want to keep to a Word file and save it that way. Otherwise, remember to carefully record all the information you find in your genealogy binder for safe-keeping. Make a note of the website where you got the information, so you can return to it if you need to.

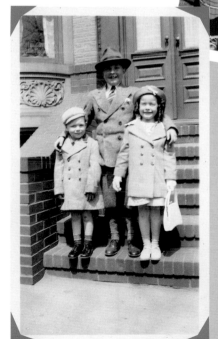

Photos from those far away remind you to keep in touch.

Showing off new spring outfits is a time-honored tradition.

Chapter 7
TRACKING YOUR ANCESTORS

WHERE ARE YOUR ANCESTORS FROM?

Part of what makes genealogy so fascinating is that you aren't just tracing your family back through time, but through place as well. You may live in America now, but only Native Americans are original natives. Everyone else came from someplace else. That could mean that you have cousins in Ireland, China, South Africa, Peru, or somewhere else in the world. On the other hand, if you live in those countries now, your family may have moved there from a different country a long time ago. Records, if they still exist, could be hard to find, or written in a different language. No matter where you are, chances are that some family members immigrated to America in the past. So whether you have lost touch with your American cousins, or want to trace your family back to the "old country," here's one place to try.

COMING TO AMERICA

Go to your computer and bring up your favorite search engine. Then type in the search phrase "Ellis Island." From 1892 to 1954, millions of people passed through the Ellis Island Immigration Center on their way to new lives in America. They sailed on ships into New York harbor from many different countries. Each person arriving on Ellis Island was given certain tests. The immigrants were examined by a doctor and given simple wooden puzzles to test their skill and intelligence. Imagine how difficult it was for people who often didn't speak the language to figure out what they were expected to do with these pieces of wood. But the immigrants came because once inside America, a whole new life awaited them.

Today, visitors come from everywhere to touch the names of ancestors etched into its "Wall of Honor." The Ellis Island website, ellisisland.org, can also help people find names on passenger lists. If your great-great-great grandfather didn't come through Ellis Island, do other searches under "immigration" (another incoming center was Angel Island in San Francisco Bay) and you just might be able to tell your grandfather something he doesn't know about his grandfather.

America became their home

- Knute Rockne, Notre Dame's famed football coach, arrived in America from Norway, in 1893.
- Frank Capra, director of the Christmas favorite "It's a Wonderful Life" emigrated from Italy in 1903.
- Entertainer Bob Hope came through Ellis Island in 1908 from England.
- Bela Lugosi, famous for playing Dracula, emigrated from Hungary in 1921.
- Science fiction writer Isaac Asimov came to America from Russia in 1923.
- The Von Trapp family, made famous by "The Sound of Music," came to America from Germany in 1938.

Were your relatives among them? How would you go about finding out? First, of course, ask your parents or older relatives. Maybe someone in your family has an old passport or some immigration papers from another country. A passport is a document issued to allow people to travel from country to country. Inside the passport booklet, look for visa stamps, those special dated markings that tell when a family member passed from one country to another. Passports usually have a photograph of the family member, too. If your family often travels together, one of your parents' passports might include you, too. Some of your relatives may have emigrated before passports were known. However, they might have been issued immigration or travel documents, and these papers will provide information that you can record in your loose-leaf workbook and onto your family tree.

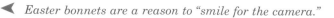

If the document includes a photo of the traveler, you'll definitely want to copy it for that family scrapbook you are working on. Adding copies of interesting visa stamps will bring your ancestors' travels to life.

WHAT'S IN A NAME?

Today more than 100 million Americans can claim an ancestor who arrived through Ellis Island. And millions of people throughout the world can claim ancestors who came to America and stayed! But finding them isn't always easy.

If you're looking for a relative with the last name of Schmidt, for example, you may not find him. His real name might have been Schmitter, or something similar. Why? Names may have been spelled incorrectly, or intentionally changed. An immigration official may have made a mistake in filling out a form, or simply misunderstood what an immigrant said. Newcomers themselves also changed their own names, wanting to "fit in." They worried that employers and others would find their foreign-sounding name hard to pronounce.

For that reason, many Asians, even today, take on new first names or nicknames, such as Tina or Harry, instead of using their birth names. Traditional Asian names are written with the surname first and the given name last: Chen (last name) Jen-Yu (first name) instead of Jen-Yu Chen. When looking up Asian names, here's a clue: the surname is almost always just one syllable, while the given name is longer.

Other ethnic groups had their own naming traditions. In Swedish tradition, a daughter of Lars who is named Christine, was called Christine Larsdatter. This was confusing to some people, so a new surname, like Olson, was selected.

Other immigrants Americanized their names: Finkelstein became Fink, the German name Schneider (meaning tailor) became Taylor, the Polish first name Wojciech changed to Albert, while the Russian Misha or Mikhail became Michael.

When doing searches, keep possible name changes, spellings, nicknames and abbreviations in mind. Frederick might be listed as Friedrich, Fred or Freddy; Richard as Ricardo or Rico; James might be given as Jimmy, or abbreviated to Jas. So, if searching for Mikhail Romanov doesn't work, for example, try Michael Romanov, Mike Romanov, or just M. Romanov. Some websites might offer alternate spellings of the name you entered, even for last names. Be sure to give these a look, too.

If, while you are doing name searches, you see a box that allows you to use something called Soundex, check it off. Soundex is a program that looks up names based on the sound of the consonants not on how the name is spelled. For example, Soundexing Clara would also bring up Klara and Claire. So, if you're unsure of the spelling of a name, use Soundex and see if the information you need comes up! Remember, part of genealogy is having hunches and making guesses, just like a detective!

A very long time ago, some people took their occupation as their surname. Henry Miller milled grains, while Tom Smith was a smithy, someone who shoed horses. If your name is Shepherd, it's possible that an ancestor may have herded sheep. Chances are your family isn't in that business anymore!

WHEN NAMES CHANGE

Many American names have foreign origins. Michelle is a French name but, since crossing the ocean, it has stayed the same. Other names, however, have changed, and knowing this can help you find your ancestors a bit more easily. Here is a name game to give you some practice. See if you can match the list of the names on the left with their correct counterparts in the right-hand column. The answer is on the next page.

Pablo	Ruth
Jacques	Anthony
Tamio	Beatrice
Maurice	Amy
Rivka	Paul
Aimee	Morris
Antonio	John
Bice	Thomas

Fun fact

America has been called the "great melting pot." What does this mean?
Think about what would happen if someone were to put crayons of all
kinds together into a pot and heat it up. The wax would melt and the
colors, shapes, and textures of all the crayons would blend together. So,
calling America a melting pot means that all the different peoples came
together and blended, creating a new mixture that is truly American!

WHO YOU ARE IS A CLUE

Where to search on the Internet for genealogical information on your family tree
depends on your ethnic background. Many African Americans today, for example, are
descendants of slaves taken from their homes along the coastline between the Congo
and Gambia Rivers in East Africa. Starting in 1619, these forced immigrants were
uprooted, transported to the Americas and the Caribbean in ships, and sold as
slaves. Most lost their proud African names to slave names, or took the plantation
owner's last name as their own. That's why, in some small rural towns in the South,
almost an entire population can have same last name. But, no matter where your
ancestors come from, or who they were, there are archives available online to help
you trace your ancestors back through several generations. One popular website,
cyndislist.com, has links to a fascinating array of archives.

FORGING CULTURAL LINKS ON THE GENEALOGY CHAIN

If you're looking for information on a missing family member, don't forget those important cultural ties. Just because people move to a new country doesn't mean they leave everything in the old culture behind. They usually arrange to live close by and get together often with people who speak the same language, eat the same foods, and enjoy the same things. Homesick for parts of the culture left behind, new immigrants stuck together and tried to recreate what was comfortable and familiar to them.

When large numbers of people were immigrating to America, little neighborhoods quickly sprang up—Chinatown, Germantown, Little Italy. You could find bagels in New York's Lower East Side, pasta in Little Italy, bratwurst in Germantown, dim sum and colorful silk clothing in Chinatown. This "coming together" of nationalities was repeated in large cities all across the country. All these cultural differences helped to make America as much of a Home Sweet Home as possible for a wonderfully diverse group of people, who simply recreated as much of their homeland as they could.

What parts of your ancestors' culture is still a part of your life? Is it your great Chinese grandmother's cold noodles and peanut sauce? Your great-great Italian grandmother's lasagna? The Greek songs your aunt sings at family gatherings? The folk dances the men in your family perform at celebrations? The piñata you break open at parties? What things in your life today are pieces of your cultural history?

Just as your mother's blue eyes might have been handed down to you, so are certain cultural traits. What did your great-grandmother teach your grandmother, who taught your mother, who taught you? These things are handed down like genes and sometimes changed. Your grandmother might have taught your mother to make her special Russian pudding with cream, but when your mother taught you, she might have used milk instead—or added raisins. How will you pass this down or change it for your children? These cultural family recipes are something you'll want to preserve by pasting them into your special family history scrapbook. You can paste your grandmother's recipe for blueberry bread into her section, and your uncle's recipe for Mexican refried beans into his.

Knowing about your ancestors' culture can help you find your ancestors, too. Look for leads to a Chinese ancestor in the Chinese community. If an Italian ancestor was famous for her pasta sauce, maybe an Italian community newspaper may have done a story on her. Whatever the nationality, local papers and community organizations are good sources of information. Maybe someone knew your grandmother when she lived in a different town. Or perhaps someone remembers the name of your grandmother's best friend. You can find wonderful clues where you never even expected to. All you have to do is ask relatives or ask people at cultural events you might attend with your family.

◄ *An old family photo might include your grandma, and her twin, as kids.*

Chapter 8
HERALDRY

IT STARTED WITH THE KNIGHTS

Have you tried to research your family name on the Internet? If so, you might have found yourself at a website that talked about heraldry, and something called a coat of arms.

Coats of arms began about a thousand years ago (the twelfth century—that means the 1100s) in Europe. It was a time when knights wore full—and very heavy—suits of armor. At a distance, or with their head armor covering their faces, it was nearly impossible to identify friend from foe. During the noise of battle, knights couldn't call out loud enough to be heard and recognized. A quick and visual way was needed to identify who was who.

So knights had identifying marks put on their shields. They wore the same design on the loose cloth cape that covered their armor to protect them from the sun's heat. The markings on the "coat" of arms allowed a knight to be recognized, even if he was separated from his shield.

Gradually, people from noble or high-class families began to use coat of arms markings. The working poor often couldn't read or write, so these "picture names" helped them, too.

Soon the identifying marks became more complex. People added symbols of honors they had won, or to commemorate important family events and special occasions. Having a coat of arms became a mark of great pride. And the status from the coat of arms was something the whole family, or clan, could share.

With so many new coats of arms being worn, and new ones being made up, a procedure was set up to register them and keep track of the many symbols that appeared on them. Even today, who is entitled to wear what on a coat of arms is strictly regulated in some countries.

Fun facts

- Lucky you, if you were the oldest son in the Middle Ages. You inherited your father's coat of arms intact. A younger son would only have a smaller picture to place in the middle of a shield.
- If you were a woman getting married, you would bring your family's coat of arms into your husband's, adding to the design.

THE COAT OF ARMS

A coat of arms is made up of several different parts. The main sections are:

1. Crest—a small simple design that originally decorated a knight's helmet. The crest alone was never meant to represent family, but it's used today to personalize stationery or to stamp a special design into envelope sealing wax.

2. Shield—a half-oval shape. Early shields often held just a simple colored pattern; later ones were divided into quarters, showing designs representing the maternal and paternal family lines.

3. Supporters—a pair of animals on either side of the shield. These family protectors were chosen for their strength, intelligence, or cunning. Lions, tigers, or bears were popular supporters.

4. Motto—a short phrase or saying. Some families today have silly mottoes like "When the going gets tough, the tough go shopping." What would be your family motto?

Biking the World

TRACING YOUR COAT OF ARMS

Do you have a coat of arms? If so, your family name may not be enough to find it. Individuals, and not families, were awarded coats of arms. So, even if your family name is not as common as Smith, you may find a choice of coats of arms given for your name.

How do you tell which one might be your family coat of arms? You would need to find out which coat of arms was granted to a particular ancestor. It may be possible to track a likely coat of arms based on where your ancestor lived. But that may not be easy. There could have been many people in that village with that same last name. And some coats of arm are listed only by country, rather than village.

If you really want to find out if an ancestor was ever awarded an actual coat of arms, search out and contact the College of Arms in your ancestor's country. You'll probably be asked for details on your genealogy and be charged a fee, but you may end up finding an official coat of arms connected to you through a family member.

SOMETHING ALL MY OWN

It wouldn't be official, but that's no reason why you couldn't make up a coat of arms of your own. What could you put on it? Just about anything. You might want to display your country's flag, and the national flags of your ancestors. You could show your ethnic pride by including a drawing of the Swiss Alps or the Great Wall of China, the "boot" shape of Italy, or a kangaroo. Even showing a food, such as two crossed crusty loaves of French bread, can represent your nationality. Family events can be drawn onto the shield: a knight with a sword, the landing of the Mayflower, the broken chains of slavery. You might choose to show the blue ribbon you won in a horse show, a skateboard because skateboarding is your favorite sport, a chess piece, musical notes or the instrument you play, or anything else that means something to you.

My Coat of Arms

Have you ever heard the expression "to come through with flying colors"? It means to hold a flag high in victory after a battle, clearly showing the winner's coat of arms. Luckily, you won't need to fight a battle. First, just create a coat of arms. Later you can make it larger, attach it to a stick, and proudly fly your own colors!

What You Need:

- paper sheets
- markers, pencils, and paints
- tracing paper
- colored construction paper
- scissors
- glue

What To Do:

1. Start with the shield. Select and trace one of the shapes given here, or draw one of your own, in the center of a sheet of paper. You can also enlarge it, or cut out a pattern, then cut a shield from heavy construction paper.

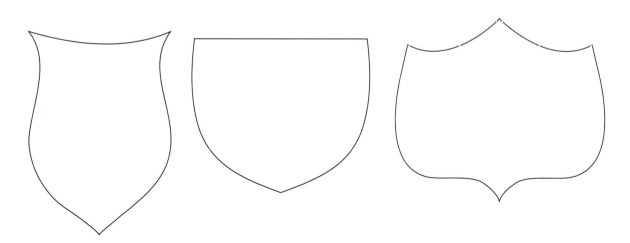

2. Draw lines to divide the shield in half, or into quarters. Use glue and construction paper or markers to add stripes of your favorite colors. Draw small pictures on your shield.

3. Draw a crest above the shield—a small and easy-to-recognize drawing to represent you, or your family.

4. If you wish, add a pair of supporters—one on each side of the shield, facing the center.

5. Think of a motto (short is best) and print it at the bottom of your coat of arms. It looks nicer on a ribbon, but you don't need one, just the motto.

Now you have a coat of arms. You can hang it on the outside of your door, or frame it to hang up in your room.

More information on heraldry and making your own coat of arms can be found at www.yourchildlearns.com/heraldry.htm.

▲ *Childhood photos like this are always nice to look back on.*

Even a simple snapshot can become a lovely family portrait. ▶

52

Chapter 9
MAKING THE CONNECTIONS

Imagine that some relatives you've never met have come to visit. Suddenly one of them steps up to you and shakes your hand. "Hi, I'm Fred Jacobs, your third cousin, twice removed."

"Huh?" You know what a cousin is, but what's a third cousin? And "twice removed?" What's that mean? Family connections can be really complicated so in genealogy, it's important to be really precise. To start, here are some handy definitions:

- First cousin—a child of your aunt or uncle.
- Second cousin—a family member who shares great-grandparents with you, but not the same grandparents.
- Third and fourth cousins—third cousins share great-great-grandparents; fourth cousins share great-great-great grandparents, and... Well, you get the idea.

"Removed" means that the two people involved are not in the same generation. For example, you and your first cousins are in the same generation, probably both about the same age. A cousin is "once removed" if that cousin is in your parents' generation. It's like moving from the children's table to the adult table at big family dinners.

FAMILY RELATIONSHIPS

Here is a chart to help you figure it out.

1. What is your relationship to the common ancestor? Find it in the row along the top of the grid.

2. What is the other person's relationship with that same common ancestor? Find it in the column down the left side.

3. Follow your row down and the other person's column across. The box where the column and the row meet in the grid tells you your relationship to that other person. For example, you are the grandchild (second column) of a common ancestor, your grandmother. You want to figure out who you are to another grandchild (second row) of that same ancestor. Match the two up on the grid! You are first cousins!

Note: In the chart opposite, G = Great.

Here's a little practice on the chart. Can you figure out these relationships?

1) You are a great-grandchild. Who are you to another great-grandchild?

2) You are a son. What relation is a great-granddaughter to you?

3) You are a great-grandchild. Who are you to a grandchild?

Answer

1) A great-grandchild and a great grandchild are second cousins.

2) A great-granddaughter and a son. The granddaughter is the son's grandniece.

3) A great-grandchild and a grandchild are first cousins once removed.

	You are					
Common Ancestor	son or daughter	grandchild	G-grandchild	G-G-grandchild	G-G-G-grandchild	G-G-G-G-grandchild
Other person						
son/ daughter	brother or sister	nephew/ niece	grand nephew or grand niece	G-grand nephew/ niece	G-G-grand nephew/ niece	G-G-G-grand nephew/ niece
grandchild	nephew or niece	1st cousin	1st cousin once removed	1st cousin twice removed	1st cousin 3 times removed	1st cousin 4 times removed
G-grandchild	grand nephew or grand niece	1st cousin once removed	2nd cousin	2nd cousin once removed	2nd cousin twice removed	2nd cousin 3 times removed
G-G-grandchild	G-grand nephew/ niece	1st cousin twice removed	2nd cousin once removed	3rd cousin	3rd cousin once removed	3rd cousin twice removed
G-G-G-grandchild	G-G-grand nephew/ niece	1st cousin 3 times removed	2nd cousin twice removed	3rd cousin once removed	4th cousin	4th cousin once removed
G-G-G-G-grandchild	G-G-G-grand nephew/ niece	1st cousin 4 times removed	2nd cousin 3 times removed	3rd cousin twice removed	4th cousin once removed	5th cousin

No one expects you to memorize all this. Just keep the chart handy (put in a bookmark). Once you really get into family relationships, it's a reference tool that can't be beat.

Chapter 10

WINDOWS ON THE PAST

One good reason to look at the past is to try to predict the future. If many people in your family have had trouble with asthma, it could mean that you and future generations will too. Many diseases are passed down through the genes. This doesn't mean that just because some family members have heart disease, everyone will. Still, it is more likely to be a problem, so extra check-ups would be a good idea. And, with today's better health care and medicines, illnesses that were once a death sentence are now curable.

TRACKING MEDICAL HISTORY

Diabetes, asthma, high cholesterol, heart disease: How can you find medical information of this kind about your family?

● A death certificate sometimes can give clues. Does it list the cause of death as heart disease or stroke?

- Relatives can sometimes provide answers. Your uncle may remember that your grandmother had terrible headaches or had to watch the sugar she ate, which would indicate diabetes.
- Obituaries can also give clues, too. If cause of death is not mentioned, a suggestion to send donations to an organization such as the Diabetes Foundation or American Heart Association would indicate what health problem that person had.

You should know that the names of many diseases have changed over time. If your great-grandmother tells you a granduncle had a terrible case of consumption, you may not have a clue what she's talking about. But you might if she called it what it is known as today: TB (for tuberculosis).

MATCH THE ILLNESS

Let's play a match game. Here is a list of health problems of years past. They're still around today, but with different names. See if you can match the old names with what they're called today, then check out your answers on the next page.

Years Past		Today
Apoplexy	___	a. heart failure
Dropsy	___	b. typhus
Glandular fever	___	c. tonsillitis
Grippe	___	d. mononucleosis
Jail fever	___	e. pneumonia
Lockjaw	___	f. flu
Quincy	___	g. stroke
Lung fever	___	h. tetanus

Apoplexy	_g_	stroke
Dropsy	_a_	heart failure
Glandular	_d_	mononucleosis fever
Grippe	_f_	flu
Jail fever	_b_	typhus
Lockjaw	_h_	tetanus
Quincy	_c_	tonsillitis
Lung fever	_e_	pneumonia

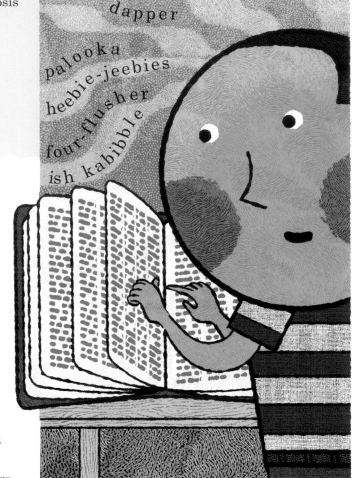

dapper
palooka
heebie-jeebies
four-flusher
ish kabibble

WORDS, LIKE FASHIONS, ALSO GO OUT OF DATE

When reading or hearing family stories, you may come across other words you don't recognize. Usually you can figure out the meaning of a word from the words surrounding it. Sometimes, it's a word you think you know, but it doesn't seem to mean what you think it does! You're at a total loss! Don't be afraid to ask questions! Sometimes the meanings of words change and some words can mean several things. It helps to try to look up strange words in a dictionary. Even slang words can be found there. Learning slang from the past is also a part of the fun of discovering your family's world.

Family Slang Dictionary

Do you use slang words when talking to friends? Well, believe it or not your parents, and their parents, did too. No wonder people of different generations don't always understand each other! Why not make a dictionary of slang words that were popular when your parents and grandparents were growing up?

What You Need:
- small notebook
- pen or pencil

What To Do:
1. Talk to your grandparents. Make up a list of words or phrases that they used to say. Write them (along with what they mean, and how they were used) in the little notebook. Some words might be "the cat's pajamas," or "groovy." Mark those pages as words your grandparents' used.
2. Now it's your parents' turn. Ask them what slang words they used to use. Write the words or phrases down on their pages along with the meanings.
3. Finally, add your own slang words to the notebook, and what you mean when you say them. Transfer the lists to the proper pages in your loose-leaf workbook, too, for safekeeping.
4. Now, look through the pages of your family slang dictionary with your parents and grandparents (and uncles and aunts, and cousins of all ages) when the family gets together. What a great way to learn to understand each other better! And someday, when future generations look at the book, they will know how to speak your "slanguage," too.

Chapter 11

THE GEOGRAPHY OF GENEALOGY

Where did your family come from? Where did they settle? Where did they move to after that? Maps can often point you in the right direction.

Old and new maps can help you track down information about your family. Actual birth, death, and property records are usually kept in state or county offices. If you have a general idea where a relative lived, a map of the area may confirm the name of the county and where records about the people who lived there may be kept. These archived records can provide all sorts of terrific information.

But don't rush off to find the latest, most complete map. Place names have been known to change over the years. Maybe a map dating back to when your relative was alive is more likely to be of help. It would show the old, original name of towns and their boundaries then. In early America, the boundary lines of townships and even states were flexible. You don't want to waste time researching a relative who, according to some record, lived in Connecticut, only to find out that the area was then a part of Rhode Island. State lines now are pretty much set, but county and town names or boundary lines are still changed or adjusted from time to time.

Could you ever imagine your great, great grand-mother on a camel!

What about world maps? Depending on where your ancestors are from, finding the proper map may even be more important. Over the years, countries have also changed names; for example, Ceylon to Sri Lanka (1972), Northern Rhodesia to Zambia (1964), and British Guiana to Guyana (1966). More recently, the countries that became part of the Union of Soviet Socialist Republics (USSR), or Russia, generations ago went back to their old names—or took on new ones—when the "Soviet bloc" broke up in 1989. And changes still go on today in various parts of the world.

Look for older maps in atlases, libraries, county or city offices, or online at historical map sites. If you can't find what you need, try looking online for information on specific place names. A search for "U.S. Place Names," for example, will bring you to a helpful site with free look-ups. Not only can you search and get information on just about every place name—you can click to see an aerial view of the site!

THE GEOGRAPHY TRAIL

Here's your chance to really play detective. Look for clues, those details in the maps, that may bring your ancestors to life. If you know an ancestor lived somewhere near Phoenix, Arizona, look for any maps that will show you, in the greatest detail, the area where your ancestor lived. Look for locations within a county. Keep an eye out for maps that show the borders of neighboring areas. Courthouses or county offices in those areas might be good places to look for information about your relatives.

Some places are very difficult to find. It's not just that they may have changed their name. Some townships were simply too small to show up on a map. Others may have died out, becoming "ghost towns" that aren't on any modern map at all. That's where old maps are helpful. You can also find lists of things like abandoned post offices, which could offer important clues for you. If you know the neighborhood or street where an ancestor lived, you may find it! Try to find a map that was created around the time your ancestor was alive. That's likely to be the most accurate and helpful. You can find this kind of map at local libraries or museums. Ask the librarian or historical society for help.

MAPS CAN TELL YOU

1. How your relatives lived

Maps can show you if an area was densely populated or rural, if there were many highways, or if it was mountainous. You can get an idea where your relatives were born, resided, attended school, worked, shopped, voted, traveled over land or water, raised families, and were laid to rest. Later maps of the

Maybe some of your ancestors grew up on a farm too.

same area might help you track down their children, and their children's children. Maybe you'll turn up some third, fourth, fifth, and sixth cousins you didn't know about.

2. What the land looked like

With certain types of maps, called "relief maps," you can see whether your relative lived in the mountains or on hilly terrain, or near small rivers or lakes. Relief maps may show conditions that would make moving or traveling to other areas difficult. Rivers that have bridges now, may not have had them when your family members lived nearby. Instead of trying to cross it, they may have traveled the river on boats because it was easier than making their way on land, through dense forests. Your ancestors may have even used the river to bring produce to market or go to school! Compare an old map to more modern ones, and you'll be able to see when and where new roads or bridges sprang up.

3. What your ancestors might have done for a living

If they lived near the ocean, maybe family members were fishermen. Turning up relatives in a mining town probably meant that they worked in the mines. People often worked where they lived, so consider each bit of information you uncover a valuable clue, and go from there. If you think an ancestor who lived in a heavily wooded area in Oregon in the early 1900s was a logger, and you haven't yet searched census records, why not try an online search for "Oregon loggers 1900s." Maybe you'll discover some interesting information on him.

4. What your ancestors did for fun

Maps can give tantalizing clues. Maybe your kin slid down grassy or snowy slopes on makeshift sleds, hiked or explored inviting caves in nearby hills, hunted in the woods, or swam in surrounding lakes. A special occasion may have meant a trip to town to catch the latest styles, or a reason to get together for a dress-up dance party. If your ancestors lived in the middle of the prairie, with no neighbors nearby, they still could have read, or made music and sung and laughed together. And at night, they might have sat outside, and pointed out pictures they imagined in the stars.

WHAT'S IN A NAME?

Many place names are similar, or even the same (the U.S. has close to 85 places called Springfield). This can make your work harder. Even if a relative mentions that his grandmother lived in Tioga County, it doesn't mean it's Tioga County, New York. There's also a Tioga County bordering it, in Pennsylvania. New Jersey alone has four different villages called Washington. Which is the one where an ancestor lived?

When faced with place names, you'll need specifics or need to dig deeper. Use any clues you may find. Maybe one village was on a rocky hillside while another bordered a lake. If an ancestor wrote in her diary, "Went swimming again this morning. I'm so happy we live near a lake!" you can smile—you've probably found the correct Washington; but check out the other two, just in case. Pulling clues together and making connections is what makes you a good detective.

Family Movement Map

So future generations can see who lived where, why not map your family's movements? When you're done, photos of the map can be tucked away for safekeeping in your big family scrapbook. Be sure to make extras. Family members will certainly be asking for copies of their own.

What You Need:
- an appropriate map
- yarn or string
- clear removable tape or pushpins
- copies of photographs
- scissors

What You Do:

1. Spread out the map and hang it against a wall.

2. Using clear tape or pushpins, affix a small photo (or photo copies) on the map where each family member lives (or lived).

3. Using a section of yarn, connect the children of a family to their parents. For example, if your great-grandparents lived in Utah, but their son moved with his family to Maine, attach a strip of yarn connecting the photo of the grandparents in Utah to the son and his family in Maine. If your family is more spread out, you can connect parents who live in Hong Kong with their five children: a son in Los Angeles, another in Sydney, Australia, and daughters in a suburb of Paris, one in Boston, and the youngest in Boulder, Colorado.

Chapter 12

FAMILY HISTORY STORIES

Have you heard the one about how your great-uncle Tom gobbled sixteen blueberry pies at a pie-eating contest and then went home and ate a full dinner? Does everyone still laugh about the how Grandma Ida Marie ran off and became a trapeze artist, then surprised everyone by becoming the toast of the town? Why do you think stories like these are repeated over and over? It's not just because they're such great stories. It's because they reveal as much about the person as a great photograph can.

Family stories can be about people doing everyday things, about their being part of great historical events, or just about places they've been and things they've seen. Such stories are just as much family heirlooms as a prized old pocket watch or a carefully preserved wedding dress.

THE STORYTELLING TRADITION

Stories from the past can affect our lives even today. Here's one about an immigrant who arrived at Ellis Island about a hundred years ago. At the time, doctors at the center examined everyone. If they were sick, the doctor chalked an X on the back of their coat. Immigrants marked with the X would be held for a short time on the island to see if they got better. If they didn't get well, they were sent back. It was a terrible thing for people who had left everything, looking for freedom and better lives in America, to be turned away.

One day, a doctor listened to an immigrant's breathing sounds. He didn't like what he heard so he quickly chalked an X on the man's back. The man knew what that meant. In a panic, he looked out across the water at the land he was so desperate to reach. Suddenly, he turned and ran, then dove straight into the water, swimming for shore!

By the time he made it ashore, the police were waiting and easily took the exhausted man into custody. He was taken to court, but the judge hearing the story was more amazed than angry. "If you're healthy enough to swim that distance, you're certainly healthy enough to make it here," he said. Then he made it official—"You can stay."

The story is a true one—a family legend of a friend of mine. Every time someone was about to give up on something they truly wanted, she tells me, the story of the grandfather who swam to shore was retold. The message was: if your grandfather could overcome great odds, so can you! It made my friend proud! And it made her feel that, just like her grandfather, she could do anything if she set her mind to it.

Family stories knit generations together. They can encourage, console, or sometimes just make you laugh. And they can make you feel closer to your ancestors.

MORE THAN A STORY

Family stories can also provide clues to finding out more information about your family. As part of a story, someone might mention the name of the town where a relative you've been searching for used to live. A story about great-grandma's prize quilt might lead you to a quilting organization with lists of present and past members online.

The collecting of family stories is sometimes called taking "oral histories," because they are verbal records of a time and a place. All this can help you in your genealogical research. You've

▲ *Clothing styles and city brownstones help to date and place a picture.*

read about World War II in your history books, but imagine how much more alive that dry information will be if you hear about it from someone who actually lived through it—someone related to you!

What will you do with these family stories? Besides helping you in your research, you may want to write out some of them and include them in your family scrapbook. For example, in her section, you might write out Grandma's story about how she met Grandpa. Or you can copy down all the stories and put them together in their own separate book. Or, if you taped the stories, you can make a new tape of all the best stories. Then make copies, or put the whole thing on CD, to give to family members.

TAKING ORAL HISTORIES

There's an art to collecting family stories. Once you have the tools: pencils, notebook, and maybe a small tape recorder, the first thing you'll need to do is know how to listen. Give all your attention to the storyteller, and don't interrupt. Save your questions for the end. Don't rush the speaker, or criticize. How would you feel if you were telling a story and someone said, "Could you tell the story a little faster?" or "This part is boring, can we skip it and get to the good parts?" Instead, say things like, "This is fascinating!" or "I could listen forever!" with an interested look on your face. It's a sure way to get the storyteller to answer your follow-up questions and want to tell you more.

MAKE UP A LIST OF QUESTIONS

Don't put someone on the spot by asking them to "Tell me a story about your life." Prepare a list of questions to help start things off. And don't forget a notebook or tape recorder to record their answers.

Here are a few starter or follow-up questions you may want to ask:

Places

1. Where did you grow up?
2. What was your house like?
3. Where did you buy your clothes or shop for food?
4. What did you do for fun where you lived?
5. Did you travel? Where? What did you see?

People

1. What were your parents like?
2. Do you remember your teachers?
3. Who did you admire most when you were growing up?
4. Who would you say played a part in changing your life?
5. Who was the first person you fell in love with and why?

In Those Days

1. Can you tell me something about when you first moved here?
2. What kind of work did you and other family members do?
3. What was going on in the world that you remember most?
4. How did what happened affect you and the family?
5. How has life changed for you since then?

Emotions

1. What story about yourself or your family makes you smile?
2. What story about yourself or your family makes you laugh?
3. What story about yourself or your family makes you cry?
4. What story about yourself or your family makes you wonder about things?
5. What story about yourself or your family makes you feel proud?

The W's of Story Writing:

The first thing news reporters learn is to answer, in their stories, the five "W"s—Who, What, Where, When, and Why. Who is telling the story? What happened in the story? Where did the story take place? When did the story take place? Why is this story important? Tag on a "How" question and you can ask just about anything (now you're on your way to becoming a news reporter).

WHAT'S YOUR STORY?

You're part of your family tree, too. So don't forget to write down your own stories. They will be memories that you can hand down to future generations. Keep them and any other family stories, in your loose-leaf workbook or put them in the family scrapbook.

◀ *Car models can help date photographs-early ones had running boards.*

Chapter 13
THE WAY THEY WERE

Were the good old days really so good?

Grandparents, and their grandparents, might have mentioned or talked at length about how much better things were in "the old days." Their memories might have softened over time—because life in the "good old days" wasn't always easy. For example:

- Frontier women did laundry by putting it in washtubs and stamping on it with their feet, pounding it with rocks on a riverbank, or scrubbing it against a washboard.
- Until as late as 1860, pigs were free to roam urban American streets. This was encouraged because they would eat the garbage left strewn all over the roads.
- Federal child labor laws were passed in 1938. Before then, children often were made to work 12 to 15 hours a day in factories. If they got hurt or couldn't work, they were quickly replaced by others who needed the jobs. Before 1900, a third of all mill hands were children.

What about life today do you think could stand improvement? Imagine how things might be in the future. For example, do you hate having to take a daily vitamin? Some day, there might be a type of "vitamin pill" given to you at birth that would take care of all your vitamin needs for your entire life!

WRITE A LETTER TO THE PAST

Pick one of your ancestors and write a letter to them. What would you say to your great-great-grandfather who came over from Poland? What would you tell him about yourself? What would you want to ask him? What do you think he would say to you?

BE A GREAT-GREAT-GREAT FOR A DAY!

Recently, a few television stations ran several so-called "reality" shows where families, or groups of strangers who agreed to take part, lived together as pioneers did hundreds of years ago. They had no running water, no electricity. They wore the same kinds of clothes and used the same tools as the pioneers did, and grew and ate the same food as in "the old days." To make things even more realistic, some were given a list of rules to follow, based on those the pioneers lived under so long ago.

Even if you didn't see these shows, you can still imagine what life was like. Think about what you have now that they didn't. You can start with running water; and not only running water but hot and cold running water!

But back then...You open your eyes and try to wake up. There's no running water but you might splash your face from a basin of cold water (of course, in winter you would first have to break the film of ice covering it)! No indoor plumbing, so you know what a hassle it would be dealing with that! And forget taking a real bath or a shower.

Now, what was life like for your great-grandparents and grandparents? That's not as long ago as pioneer days, but what do you suppose they had at your age?

- Pen and ink or fountain pens, then ball points; no markers or highlighters or gel pens.
- Telegraph or dial-up telephones; definitely no wireless, or take-everywhere cell phones!

- Radio programs (think TV drama, sit-coms, concerts without a picture); no recorded music or call-in talk shows
- Wind-up, then thankfully, electric phonographs playing 78 rpm (revolutions per minute) records with one song on each side, then albums at 45 and 33 1/3rd rpm. No music-to-go, available 24/7.
- Silent movies, talkies, 3-D, stereo-sound, and wide-screen. Movie theater give-away nights and family car drive-ins. No DVDs to bring the theater experience right into your home.
- Propeller-driven planes, steam trains, automobiles with sideboards, trailers, but no vans or SUVs.
- Black-and-white TV, then color; no flat, wide, and hang-on-your-wall screens with news instantly "beamed in" from around the world.
- Manual, then electric typewriters; now, personal computers and printers, fax machines, digital cameras, even cell phones that take pictures, all unknown to your grandparents in "their day," are there for you today.

In the kitchen, your grandmother's mother probably had a wood- or oil-burning stove and an "ice-box" to keep things cold (the melting ice collected in a pan underneath and would overflow if she didn't empty it in time). For entertainment, books were always around, but forget computer games. Games were on boards and meant for two (chess, checkers) or a whole family to play together. Early TV had only a few channels, and programs were on for only a few hours a day. The shows were "live" so if someone made a mistake or something unexpected happened (think "Funniest Home Videos") everyone who was tuned in saw it! No hundred channels coming into your home by cable or bounced off satellites! No pictures sent back from cameras launched into outer space or "rovered" around on nearby planets.

Girls, you wouldn't be deciding what you wanted to be when you grow up. You were expected to marry and stay home, keeping house and taking care of your family while your husband went out to work. Your days would be spent canning, cooking, washing, ironing, and sewing. Of course, many of those things are still done today, but time-saving devices (washer/dryers, microwave ovens, sewing machines) have made things a lot easier. Now, people have the right to decide for themselves what they want to do with their lives and see how far they can go—whether it's to win gold medals at the Olympics, be the first one in the family to get a Ph.D. degree, or fly to Mars.

Yes, things have changed a lot over the years from your grandmother to you. Can you even imagine what things your grandchildren will see when you reach the age your grandmother is now? What will the world be like in your children's future?

Genealogical timeline

Things are constantly changing, and it's hard to imagine what effect these changes had on your ancestors and older family members. Sometimes, to understand things, it helps to see them. Since your family stretches back through time, you can get a better picture of their life changes by making a genealogical timeline.

What You Need:

- photographs, news clippings, historical items
- lightweight clothesline or twine
- small paper clips
- colored yarn or ribbon
- stick-on labels

What to Do:

1. Gather some family photos, or make copies. You'll want pictures of your grandparents from babyhood to the present, of your mom and dad, and of yourself, too. Look for house photos: the one your great-grandparents lived in, the one your grandparents lived in and, finally, the house you live in now. If you want more, consider photos of family pets through the years, the cars your family owned, groups at special occasions, even favorite toys.

2. Put all the pictures in order chronologically, meaning the oldest ones first.

3. Tie a length of clothesline, twine, or ribbon so it stretches across a wall of your room. This is your basic timeline.

4. Divide the timeline into time periods by tying and hanging down some colored yarn or ribbon to represent time periods of ten, twenty-five, or fifty years. Tie them loosely so that space can be adjusted based on the number of photographs you want to hang.

5. To make the timeline's years easier to see, write the time periods (1920s, for example) on labels and attach them to the hanging markers.

6. Clip each photo from the pile onto the timeline, starting at the left: Your grandfather as a young boy. The year he was twenty-two. Your mom when she was five, and when she and your dad got married. Adjust the positions and time period markers as you go to fill the timeline with photographs.

7. If there's room, add historical information such as special dates, illustrations, and clippings from books. For example, if a relative fought in World War II, attach photographs or newspaper items about the war in that space on the timeline.

What did they do before these popular inventions? Ask your mom, dad, grandparents, and great-grandparents:

ballpoint pen	1938	credit card	1950	roller blades	1979
Band-Aids	1920	crossword puzzle	1913	spiral notebook	1924
bar-code scanner	1969	hula hoop	1958	teabag	1904
		jet engine	1930	3-D movies	1922
bubble gum	1928	Post-it notes	1974	zipper	1913

Chapter 14
FAMILY TRADITIONS

A tradition can be anything from going to Midnight Mass on Christmas Eve each year to always saying "bunny, bunny, bunny" for good luck when you wake up. What traditions have been handed down in your family?

Many families have a tradition of eating dinner together. It's a chance to talk over what happened during the day, or to air out problems. One friend took part in "family night." Her father would read something aloud and the family would discuss it and use it as a stepping-stone to more conversation. Another family I know had "game night." They would pull out a favorite board game, put out bowls of snacks, and sit around the table and play together. What do you think would be a great activity for your family to do every week? Go bowling? Cook dinner together?

If you do start a new family tradition, maybe it will still be going strong when your grandchildren are your age.

CELEBRATION TIME!

What does your family celebrate? Christmas, Hanukkah, or Kwanza? A friend of mine picks up a small evergreen tree each year and decorates it with dreidels and Stars of David instead of Christmas balls. Or maybe your family celebrates Ramadan, Cinco de Mayo, or Asian New Year. The calendar is full of special days and opportunities for celebrating—and for starting new traditions.

The birthday cake was a new tradition a little over two hundred years ago. It started in Germany as a cake of sweetened bread dough. Birthday candles were lit so the smoke, on blowing them out, would carry your unspoken wish up to the gods.

So why not come up with your own family reason for celebrating, and schedule it every year on a certain date. It could be as simple as, every spring, planting marigolds in a small portion of your backyard to celebrate new life. The choices are as open as your imagination!

TRADITIONAL FOODS

Certain foods are traditional for special holidays: hamentashen, cookies shaped like little 3-sided hats celebrate the Jewish holiday of Purim. Christmas cookies are flat shapes decorated with red and green sugar, while turkey and cranberry sauce is fine for Thanksgiving feasting. Countries around the world have traditional foods for holidays and family meals. If your ancestors lived in the South, chances are they ate

more sweet potato pie, grits, and collard greens than their relatives in Boston, who tended toward Boston baked beans and Boston cream pie.

HOME COOKING?

"It's just like mother used to make." How many times have you heard someone say that? Yes, holidays are good reasons for special fancy meals, and old fashioned home cooking often deserves the highest praise any meal can get! It means food that's cooked with love and with care. And special recipes often have secret ingredients that are handed down from generation to generation. It's a great way to keep in contact with your ancestors. Make your great great-great grandmother's brownies the way she did, and you are recreating a part of your past!

Back when people didn't have cookbooks or the Internet to look for recipes, they wrote them out and handed them out, often on index cards, as gifts. My mother's recipe cards were often faded and worn from use. We looked forward to those family favorites. Why not make your own recipe box and stock it with your family's favorite recipes?

Collect every recipe you can find that has been handed down by family members (ask if they have more) and make a special family recipe box to hold them. Do some research and you may even find some recipes that an ancestor might have enjoyed. Then title them with zingy names such as Aunt Martha's Marvelous Munchy Candy Mounds, Uncle Bob's Spicy-Licious Barbeque Sauce, or Cousin Irma's Devilishly Delicious Devils' Food Cake.

Recipe Box

When you're in a mood to cook, it's great to have your family's favorite recipes all in the same place. So now's the time to get started on this kitchen project.

What To Do:

- photo storage or shoe box
- magazine clippings of anything to do with food. (Cut out pictures, and even lettering, to decorate your box with "Good Eating!" or "What's Cooking?")
- scissors
- white glue
- plastic dish
- soft brush
- tempura paint
- colored index cards to fit box

What To Do:

1. First, paint your box a bright color. Be sure to let it dry completely!
2. Select pictures and lettering, and decide on a pattern.
3. Pour some glue into a plastic dish. Use a soft brush to apply the glue to the back of your paper cutouts and put them in place on the box.

4. Once the glue has dried, apply a thin layer of glue all over the box.

5. While the box is drying, write out or glue recipes on the cards—longer recipes both front and back, or on two or more cards stapled together.

6. Put the recipes in your box.

Fun Facts

- Apples have been around for many years, but applesauce wasn't invented until 1390.
- The first potato chips (fried potatoes cut "thin") were made in 1853.
- It was at the 1904 World's Fair in St. Louis that ice cream and waffles were brought together-and the ice-cream cone was born.
- Believe it or not, none of your relatives tasted Jell-O® before 1910. That's when the quivering dessert was first invented.

FAMILY SONGS

In the Appalachian Mountains, there is a tradition called "song catching." For years before the invention and popular use of tape recorders, people would "catch" songs. They were sung over and over until a younger person memorized them. In this way, their songs were passed down from generation to generation, in much the same way as oral histories were. Of course, as people took turns singing the songs, they sometimes changed them. A young woman with a nice soprano voice might have added some high trills, while an expert banjo player put in extra chords and harmonies. One singer probably sang a tune softly, while another sang out gleefully. It may have been the same song, but people sang it differently.

Historical events have also led to other kinds of songs. During World War II everybody, including your relatives, were probably singing along to the morale building "Boogie Woogie Bugle Boy from Company B," made famous by the Andrews Sisters. Another song, dating from the Revolutionary War, is still known today as "Yankee Doodle." The song was actually written by the British, making fun of the colonists as know-nothing bumpkins! Instead of getting upset, the colonists took the song as their own and sang it with pride. What songs do you suppose your ancestors sang and what did the songs mean to them? Ask your older family members to sing some traditional songs that they remember from their childhood. Maybe you can "catch them." Or make a whole tape of traditional songs.

TAPE SOME FAVORITES

Get in tune with the songs that have been enjoyed by family members over the years. Does your Mom sing along to those "old" folk tunes her mother loved to sing, so you've learned the words, too? Does your Granddad suddenly stop talking to listen intently whenever he recognizes the great tenor voice of Pavarotti on a classical radio station? Maybe jazz, hip-hop, big band, rock-and-roll, or today's popular music is always playing in some room of your house, or through private earphones. If everybody marches to the beat of a different drummer, why not do some research and make up a "sampler" of favorites. Include something for everybody, from your Mom and Dad's special song, that they danced to at their wedding, to the tune that Grandma sings softly whenever she is sitting with her new grandchild. Set the sampler tape or CD playing at your next family barbecue or get-together, and you'll probably hear Grandpa Garcia, or Aunt Dorothy, or cousin Angelo say, "Listen, that's my favorite song." It's certainly something you'll want to keep, to remember everyone by for many years to come.

▲ *Bathing suits covered much more than they do today.*

80

Chapter 15
A FAMILY REUNION!

$\mathcal{N}$ ow that you've gotten to know your whole family better, why not celebrate by helping them all get to know each other better, too? The best way to do this is with a family reunion. When's the last time you got together with your family? Thanksgiving dinner? New Year's Eve? When was the last time you saw ALL of your family—the aunts, cousins, nephews and second and third and even fourth cousins, too? A year ago at your Aunt Ray's wedding? Two years ago? Some families have yearly family gatherings where hundreds of members come together for picnics or parties.

Whether you make it a yearly event or a once-in-a lifetime celebration, having a family reunion is a great way for members to keep in touch. And what's more fun than a party? Although there's a lot you can do on your own, you're going to need the help of your parents for this.

First, what kind of party should you have? Give it some thought. A big picnic at the park? A barbecue in the backyard? Or will you need to rent a hall someplace? What is decided, once your parents sign on to the idea, will depend on the size of your family, the cost, when the reunion is scheduled, and what kind of things your family enjoys. Are you all beach-lovers? Or do you enjoy dressing up for formal occasions? Like jazz or classical music, or none at all? Does your family quickly line up for hotdogs and burgers from a grill, or prefer to sit down to a meal? Should you hire a DJ or live band, or can family members provide their own musical entertainment? These are all things to take into consideration.

TIME TO SEND OUT INVITATIONS

You've got a go for the party? Good! Now, start by making up a list of those to be invited. Check it out with your parents, because you don't want to forget anyone. Some family members may live across the country, even halfway around the world. Some may have other things scheduled, so can't come. Still, they should be invited— and you may be pleasantly surprised to see them turn up or prepare something on their own to join in the family fun!

Family Reunion Invitation

With many people to invite, it's a good idea to design and print up your own invitations. If you have a home computer, you might have a program that makes up cards so you can print them off on your own color laser printer! If not, it is perfectly fine to design a simple single-sheet invitation, to be taken and photocopied in black and white or in color.

What You Need:

- paper
- pens
- markers
- clippings
- access to photocopier
- envelopes to fit

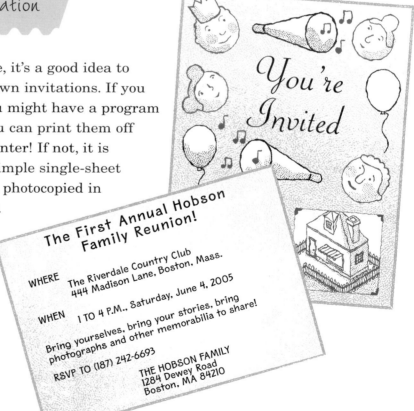

The First Annual Hobson Family Reunion!

WHERE   The Riverdale Country Club
444 Madison Lane, Boston, Mass.

WHEN   1 TO 4 P.M., Saturday, June 4, 2005

Bring yourselves, bring your stories, bring photographs and other memorabilia to share!

RSVP TO (187) 242-6693

THE HOBSON FAMILY
1284 Dewey Road
Boston, MA 84210

What To Do:

1. First, decide what you want your invitation to look like. The cover could say something as simple as YOU'RE INVITED!

2. On a computer, you might scan and show a family photo; a single sheet can hold drawings or glued-on art.

3. Next, you want to give the occasion a name (The First Annual Hobson Family Reunion!), tell them where it will be (The Riverdale Country Club, 444 Madison Lane, Boston, Mass.), and when it will be (1 to 4 pm, Saturday, June 4, 2006).

4. Add a line suggesting what family members might bring, such as: Bring yourselves, your favorite stories, a family potluck with recipe. Bring special photographs and significant objects and other memorabilia to share.

5. Print the letters RSVP and your phone number. RSVP stands for the French "Repondez s'il vous plait" and asks that the person call and let you know if they will be coming or not.

Once the invitation is finished, you're ready to have as many cards or sheet invitations printed off as you need. Then all you have to do is address and stamp the envelopes, stuff them, and get them in the mail.

A REAL FAMILY MEAL

Remember when you were collecting all those recipes for your recipe box and cook-book? Now is the time to ask family members who will be coming to make and bring their own family recipe to share. Check with them to see what, if anything, they will be able to bring. You will want to have a good selection of foods available, especially if certain family members have food allergies or need a special diet. Make up a list to see if you need another main dish, or salad or dessert, then check your family recipe box for something you would like to try—if you haven't already. If you're not an experienced cook, trying something new can be a challenge. Don't be afraid to ask your parents for help. After all, they are family, too!

DECK THE HALLS!

To start things rolling, you might want to have a table set up where people can put the significant objects they brought with them. Your Great-aunt Ethel's first pair of roller skates, that comes with a key! The cloth doll your great-grandmother handed down to Aunt Takako. Your own first pair of baby shoes! As people arrive, they can put more and more interesting things on the table.

AND HERE'S...THE FAMILY!

Bring out the results of your family research, and get ready for smiles:

● Your genealogical timeline—if you can't move it out of your room for the great day, you'll just have to clean up your room and invite everyone in.

● Your own family tree and genealogical loose-leaf binder—it's a good time for relatives to check over name spellings, dates, and facts. Keep a small notebook and pencil handy for any details to be changed or followed-up on.

● Your traditional and "sampler" tapes, and some albums with songs from the different decades (your parents probably have some put aside)—anybody want to sing along?

● Your oral history tape, along with written copies of favorite family stories— maybe they'll inspire a few more family members to tell stories of their own.

● Your family recipe box with favorite recipes—did anyone bring new old favorites?

● Your family scrapbook—by now you should have many pages in it, filled with photos, recipes, and facts, facts, facts.

FAMILY PHOTO SPOT

You'll want to have a place where your reunion guests can enjoy looking over some family photos—and maybe add a few of their own. Maybe you can move your genealogical timeline from your room to the living room and leave room underneath for another line to hold photos brought by family members. If that doesn't work, put up a single line, or some shorter ones, to hang guests' photos. Attach a few pictures to start, and show what the lines are for, then leave a basket nearby with clips for your guests to use.

If there's no room for lines of photographs, set up a few cork bulletin boards. Keep pushpins handy for people to tack up any photos they brought. (If you place a pushpin off the top edge of a photo and another off the bottom edge, it can be hung without having to puncture the photograph itself.) Put out stick-on labels, pens and markers, and encourage your guests to label and identify people and places in the photos.

LET THE FESTIVITIES BEGIN!

People coming to the reunion will bring their photos or tell stories about the people and places that mean something special to them, like the covered bridge where Grandpa proposed to Grandma! Big sister might bring her favorite Barbie, the one she got when she was six. Compare and contrast! How much have things changed. How have they stayed the same? Bring your treasures and memorabilia, too. It's show-and-tell time for everyone!

For "who's who" fun, post a variety of pictures on a bulletin board and, underneath, reveal who it is and when the photo was taken. Keep pictures of close family members together, so people can see who looks like whom. Be sure to have a group of "you must have been a beautiful baby" shots, with photos nearby of the same people as adults. See if everyone can match the baby pictures with the grown-ups they are today.

WE'VE GOT GAMES!

Make sure you have plenty of things to do to keep the party rolling. One activity is to get everyone together for a "when I was a girl / when I was a boy" game. It's more fun when relatives of all ages (great-grandma to just-turned-teen) play. For this game, you need to prepare in advance a dozen or more slips of paper with a single question written on each. In turn, each person is asked to select a paper from the "hat," think back to when they were about 8 to 12 years old, and answer the question. Others playing the game can chime in with their answers and comments—but they still have to "select a paper" on their turn!

Here are a number of questions and requests to start you off. Add more of your own if you wish, but it's best to keep things general. You don't want to embarrass anyone.

- Who was really, really famous then and why?

- What was your favorite candy?

- What did you really love to wear?

- Sing the first two lines of your favorite song?

- Where did you like to go on summer vacations?

- What game did you like to play?

- What kind of pet did you have and why?

- What gift did you receive that was "special"?

- What movie did you go to see several times?

- Recite something that you learned in school.

- Who was President, and what was happening in the world?

- What TV or radio show did you always listen to?

- What was your favorite home-cooked meal?

- When you "went out" what was it you did?

- What happened to you that seems funny to you now,
  but maybe wasn't then?

REMEMBER FAMILY PHOTOS!

Don't forget to have a couple of film or digital cameras so you or others can record this very special day. Check beforehand that the cameras are working and the film and batteries are fresh. If you have a video cam, play reporter and focus on as many family members as you can. Let each guest say a few words into the camera: Who they are. Where they are from. What family means to them. If there's no video cam, guests can still be photographed and asked to "say a few words" on audiotape. If you have your notebook handy, you might want to jot down a word or two to remind you to follow up on something. But don't try to write everything down, you won't have time. And you want to enjoy the family reunion, too!

The most important thing is, don't forget to take several photos of the whole entire clan! If you have a big family, now is a good time to gather outside, providing the weather is reasonable, and line up-shorter people, sitters and kneelers in front. (Ask if everyone can see the camera.) Maybe you can have a photographer come by, or a neighbor who is handy with a camera can take few shots—and a few more "just in case"—so nobody in the family will be left out of these very special photos.

Chapter 16
KEEPING IN TOUCH

Just because the reunion is over, doesn't mean the good times have to stop. There are lots of ways you can still keep in touch and share! Treasure your First Annual Family Reunion by gathering photos and preserving all those terrific memories for the next family get-together. Find the best photo of the whole family. Scan it onto thank-you cards, or have copies of the photo made to send to everyone. Photos can also be sent to those who didn't come—maybe next year, they'll be the first to arrive for the fun!

START A FAMILY NEWSLETTER

In the meantime, a newsletter is a great way for a family to keep in touch and share news. You can take your list of all the people you invited to the reunion, including the ones who weren't able to come, and turn it into a newsletter mailing list. When would you send out your newsletter? Maybe once a year at holiday time? Midway between family reunions? Maybe even twice a year, six months apart? What will you call the newsletter? How about *The _____ Family Bugle?*

The most important details are: What is the newsletter going to say? How will you get the "news" for the newsletter?

Before you even think of that first issue, send a brief note to everyone telling them that you are starting a family newsletter. Ask that whenever they have news to report, or have family photos taken, they e-mail (if you have e-mail) or snail mail them to you! Tell them that you'd like to know things such as:

- Did anything special happen recently?

- How has the year been for you?

- What were the good things that happened?

- Did any bad things happen, that you want to tell us about?

- If you go to work, did anything interesting happen on the job?

- If you are in school, what are you studying?

- What movies did you see this year? Which ones did you especially like?

- What books did you read this year? What was your favorite and why?

- Did you watch any sports? Which teams do you root for?

Include questions on any other topics you'd like to hear about—most likely others in the family would also enjoy hearing. Then, gather up all the responses, put them in a folder, and refer to them when you write the text of your newsletter. Remember: try to include in the item as many answers as possible to: Who, What, Where, When, Why, and How. That's what the readers of your newsletter are going to want to know. Also, try to include as many different relatives in each newsletter as you can—so that they can look for mentions of themselves as well as catching up on other family members.

Next, you have to decide what your newsletter will look like. Will it be a hand-printed sheet that you photocopy, or a page or two printed out by computer on colored sheets of paper, or a file sent by e-mail? Do you want to include photographs? Do you want a "Good News" section? Do you want to share recipes? How about information on favorite travel spots? Maybe you want to add some original poems and stories, too. And don't forget items about the last family reunion, or reminders about the next family reunion you might be planning!

LAUNCH A FAMILY WEBSITE

Whatever you can do with a newsletter, you can arrange to do on a website. With your family's permission and help, the right computer software, and some technical know-how, you might be able to get a website up and running yourself. Otherwise, there are books available to tell you what to do and how to do it, and websites that can help you set one up—or set it up for you. A website can be as creative and unique as you like, show photographs in full color, and even include short videos or animation. Since websites can be accessed from around the world, family members don't have to live right next door anymore, or down the block, or even in the next township over. People can live anywhere around the world and still be...family!

◄ *Lucky you, if a sign tells where a photo was taken.*

And you ► thought great grandpa only used a cane as he got older!

Chapter 17
BACK TO THE FUTURE

It's been fun, and through genealogy, you've gotten to know your whole family better, maybe going back to long before you were born. Now, what would you like family members still to come—your children, your children's children, and great- and grandnephews and nieces—to know about you? Why not put together a personal time capsule? You can leave them all a unique message that says, "Hello!" What better way is there to bring your whole family— past, present, and future members—together?

91

A "My time" Capsule

The hardest part of a time capsule is deciding what to put inside. But whatever you do, don't forget to include copies of your family tree research. You'll be saving your descendants from having to do all that information gathering all over again.

What You Need:

- a container (coffee can, cookie tin, small box, plastic bag or wrapping)
- markers
- items that say "my time"
- a safe place

What do you think your great-great grandkids would want to know about you and your time? What will you put in?

1. Photos: Put together a small photo album showing your family at work and play—how they live and dress. Label or caption each photo with the person's name and date, and where the photo was taken. Remember to include pictures of yourself, your friends, your room—after all, this is your capsule!

2. Clothing: What are the latest styles? Put in a pair of those squiggly laces you like for sneakers. Show you're a fan—include a baseball cap naming your favorite team.

3. Technology: You may not want to put in your prized MP3 player, but you can tuck in a photo and description of it and how much it cost. Cut out ads with prices for other "wish list" items—in the far future, they may not even be a memory.

4. Food: Avoid treating generations of ants to your favorite candy bar—a neatly flattened wrapper or two will do. What do you like to eat? Add a list. Maybe the finder of your time capsule will have the same taste in foods.

5. Newspapers: Today's headlines! Newspaper decays, so protect paper items in heavy plastic, or laminate clippings that mean something special to you and your family.

MORE STUFF FOR YOUR TIME CAPSULE

Want to get closer to your family to come? Maybe some day you'll sit in a rocker and tell your grandkids stories about when you were their age. Maybe even your great-grandchildren. But your time capsule may not be found until after you're gone, and you're living it now. So, here's your chance. Write a letter to those future generations.

Here's an example:
Dear great, great, great, great grandkids,
My name is Elaine. It's 2003 and I'm eleven. George W. Bush is President. Living in Boston is lots of fun because there's so much to do: museums and shopping and movies and just hanging out and playing Frisbee in the Boston Commons. I intend to be an award-winning scientist when I grow up.

TAKING THE GRAND TOUR

In the 1960s, Jacqueline Kennedy, the wife of President John F. Kennedy, gave TV viewers a historic guided tour of the White House. Why not treat your grandkids, or great-great grandkids, to a guided tour of the place you call home?

Do you have a video or regular camera? Buy, borrow, or rent one and produce your own tour. Start from the outside of your house and work your way in. Label your photos, or write or talk about what each room is used for—here's where I beat my brother at chess. Here's where my mother writes her novels. Point out interesting facts. This is the desk where I wrote my first short story! Here's where I go when I'm in a bad mood and want to be by myself. Make the tour as personal as you'd like—it's in the family, after all.

DO NOT OPEN UNTIL...

Assemble everything into your time capsule. Identify it and mark it with a "Do not open until" date: 20 years from now, 30 years, maybe 50 years. Even New Year's Eve of the year 3000 (although you may not be around to see it)! On your genealogy page in your loose-leaf notebook, make a note about the time capsule (the date you made it up and where you put it) so that it is not forgotten and lost forever. Make sure that it is properly protected, and then put it away somewhere.

Where will you put your time capsule?

- In the backyard: If you bury it, draw yourself a map to remind yourself where it is. Protect the time capsule from water and other damage by wrapping it in strong plastic bags or sheeting.
- Hidden under a staircase, or behind a loose board in a wall: Out of sight, out of mind.
- In the attic: Put it out of the way, so it isn't accidentally tossed out the next time Mom or Dad has a cleaning fit up there.
- In your closet: You can keep an eye on it there, but snoopy siblings may get curious.

A PEEK AT THE FUTURE

Just as you've discovered generations of your family going back a hundred or so years, there probably will be generations of your family going forward many years. Can you imagine that!

In *The Time Machine,* written by H. G. Wells, a man invents a machine to travel into the future. He remains in one place, sitting in the time machine in the basement of his house. Through his basement window, he can see a dummy in the window of a shop nearby. As he is "traveling," he watches the hem of the mannequin's dress get shorter, then longer, then shorter, then wider—as styles change through the years. Suddenly, the little shop window disappears—and he's there in the future!

Imagine your own home. Will it still be there in 20 years? Or 50 years? What will things be like in 100 years? Will houses be built on the ground, under ground, or stretch way up into the sky? Will there be speedy flyers hovering around, instead of streets and long highways filled with cars?

Imagine you are all grown up and married. What does your wife or husband look like? What kind of work do you do? What do your kids look like? Do people tell you that your children have your same crooked smile? Do your kids have a dog or a cat like you used to at their age? Did you just remember the date you put on your time capsule? Now imagine four and five generations of your family getting together someday at reunions—one that you started!

AFTERWORD

PLANT IT, IT'S YOUR FAMILY TREE

Part of what makes genealogy so much fun is that it keeps growing and changing before your very eyes. Everything you learn about your family adds to it. Your family is a vibrant and living thing, and what better way to symbolize it than with a living and growing tree?

Go to a local nursery and ask someone there to help you select a tiny seedling that will grow well for you. Get planting and growing instructions to take with you. When you get home, plant the tree right away. You may have a nice place selected in front of your house, or in your backyard. A very large pot on a porch or patio might do for a while, but a tree belongs in the ground. Its roots need room and nourishment in order to grow tall, and the branches and leaves of most trees will want to spread out. Care for your family tree and watch it grow from year to year. Every time you look at it, you'll be reminded of the wonderful living, growing thing each and everyone's family truly is.

INDEX